Praise for 61 Humorous & Inspiring Lessons I Learned From Baseball By Howard Kellman

"Howard Kellman brings a wealth of personal experience in writing these gems. No one I know, in or out of baseball, has a keener recall of events than Howard does."
-Carl Erskine, former Dodgers All-Star Pitcher

"A great and quick read for baseball fans and non-baseball fans. Some poignant stories with a nice touch of humor. Easy to read and hard to put down."
-Larry Rothschild, Chicago Cubs Pitching Coach

"What a fun book! Having covered thousands of baseball games for the Indianapolis Indians, Howard Kellman must have nearly that many stories he could share. You are certain to enjoy the 61 he has chosen to include in this book."
-Randy Mobley, President, International League

61 Humorous & Inspiring Lessons I Learned From BASEBALL

Howard Kellman

authorHOUSE

AuthorHouse™
1663 Liberty Drive
Bloomington, IN 47403
www.authorhouse.com
Phone: 1-800-839-8640

© 2010 Howard Kellman. All rights reserved.

No part of this book may be reproduced, stored in a retrieval system, or transmitted by any means without the written permission of the author.

First published by AuthorHouse 4/2/2010

ISBN: 978-1-4490-9986-2 (e)
ISBN: 978-1-4490-9984-8 (sc)

Library of Congress Control Number: 2010903631

Printed in the United States of America
Bloomington, Indiana

This book is printed on acid-free paper.

Cover photo: Roger Maris, following through on his swing, after batting his 61st home run at Yankee Stadium, October 1, 1961. Anthony Bernato, photographer.
Used by permission (copyright) 2002 – 2010 by Corbis Corporation.
All visual media (copyright) by Corbis Corporation and/or its media providers.
All rights reserved.

To my wife, Robin, for all her love and support; she, more than anyone else, helped to bring this book to publication

*In memory of my parents,
for their love and support*

Contents

Foreword xi
A Special Dedication to Ernie Harwell......................xiii
Introduction... xv

THE 61 LESSONS

Lesson 1.	Getting A "Good Jump" Can Be Meaningless 1	
Lesson 2.	There Are Times To Instill Confidence.......3	
Lesson 3.	Being Nice Has Its Benefits 5	
Lesson 4.	Given Guidance, Young Players Can Improve Dramatically 7	
Lesson 5.	There Are Many Roads To Cooperstown..10	
Lesson 6.	Time Does Not Heal All Wounds............12	
Lesson 7.	Don't Share Your Thrills With Everyone...14	
Lesson 8.	Sometimes You Should Give Less Than 100% 16	
Lesson 9.	Some Potential Can Be A Very Good Thing..18	
Lesson 10.	Your Thoughts Can Come Back To Haunt You 20	
Lesson 11.	He Was Much More Than A Pioneer........23	
Lesson 12.	Encouragement Has Many Faces...............26	
Lesson 13.	Determination And Resiliency Are An Unbeatable Combination 28	

Lesson 14. A Teacher Can Help Push You To Greatness 30
Lesson 15. Trouble Can Come From Strange Places .. 32
Lesson 16. Being Polite Does Not Always Work 34
Lesson 17. Sometimes You Can't Please Anyone 36
Lesson 18. Not Everyone Wants To Be Encouraged ... 38
Lesson 19. Young Players Need Guidance 41
Lesson 20. The Greats Adjust In Due Time 43
Lesson 21. There Is More Than One Way To Make Your Point 45
Lesson 22. Games Can Be Cancelled For Many Reasons 47
Lesson 23. Shared Knowledge Can Bring Success 49
Lesson 24. Some People Talk Yet Never Say Anything 51
Lesson 25. Christopher Columbus Discovered More Than America 53
Lesson 26. Be Careful - You Never Know With Whom You Are Speaking 55
Lesson 27. Intra-squad Games Can Have Incredible Ramifications 57
Lesson 28. When Pitch Comes To Shove, Humor Is The Answer 59
Lesson 29. The Great Ones Will Even The Score 62
Lesson 30. It Takes Time To Become A "Big Unit" ... 63
Lesson 31. You Had Better Be Thorough 66
Lesson 32. If You Are Going To Do Something, Make Note Of It 68
Lesson 33. There Are Different Kinds Of Pressure 70

Lesson 34.	Never Mess With Your Manager	72
Lesson 35.	Don't Take Anything For Granted	74
Lesson 36.	Bosses Can Be Outsmarted	76
Lesson 37.	Some Nicknames Are Well Earned	78
Lesson 38.	Exhibition Games Are Very Important To Some People	80
Lesson 39.	You Can't Win Some Arguments	82
Lesson 40.	Radar Guns Can Be Overrated	83
Lesson 41.	Attitude Is The Most Important Word In The English Language	85
Lesson 42.	Don't Saddle Yourself With Limitations	87
Lesson 43.	Don't Make Promises You Don't Intend To Keep	89
Lesson 44.	There Is Much Help Behind The Scenes	91
Lesson 45.	Some Home Runs Can Be Bigger Than All Of Us	93
Lesson 46.	Let Mechanics Work On Cars	95
Lesson 47.	The Explanation Is In The Eye Of The Beholder	97
Lesson 48.	Watch Your Words So You Won't Have To Eat Them	99
Lesson 49.	There Are Different Ways Of Saying A Player Can't Miss	101
Lesson 50.	Being Critical Of Others Can Create Problems For Yourself	103
Lesson 51.	Business Before Anything Including Patriotism	105
Lesson 52.	There Are Different Perspectives On Tardiness	107

Lesson 53. You Must Go With Your Strengths 109
Lesson 54. Don't Try To Be A Hero 111
Lesson 55. A Bunt Can Do Wonders 113
Lesson 56. Hitters Bring A Different Perspective 115
Lesson 57. Savor The Moment 117
Lesson 58. Foul Balls Can Put Some People In A
            Foul Mood 119
Lesson 59. Teamwork Is The Essence Of Life 121
Lesson 60. A Baby's Arrival Can't Be Predicted 124
Lesson 61. A "Moose" Can Save The Day 126
Acknowledgements 129

Foreword
By Ernie Harwell

Howard Kellman knows.

He knows baseball. He knows baseball broadcasting. He knows how to tell baseball stories. And he knows how to write about the game.

He proves all of this in his delightful and entertaining book, <u>61 Humorous & Inspiring Lessons I Learned From Baseball</u>. The book is a great example of Howard's talented authorship and his love and dedication to baseball. His anecdotes are informational and educational – packed with humor and inspiration.

I first met Howard during the baseball strike of 1981. Since there were no Tigers games for Paul Carey and me to broadcast on WJR, the station assigned us to cover the Tigers' Minor League team in Evansville, Indiana. The Evansville team played Indianapolis. Kellman had been the voice of the Indianapolis Indians for six years at that time. I found him to be warm and engaging. We became great friends. I have enjoyed following his outstanding 34 year career.

I certainly enjoyed this book. I felt that I was sitting in a clubhouse or in a dugout, having a delightful conversation with my very close friend. I'm sure that you will feel the same way.

January 4, 2010

A Special Dedication to Ernie Harwell

Ernie Harwell was kind enough to write the foreword for this book in January, 2010. He is a close friend and mentor; one who is extremely thoughtful and considerate.

I called Ernie on Labor Day of 2009, to plan our next visit. He asked that I come to see him within the next two weeks. Ernie recently had been hospitalized and had been diagnosed with a very aggressive form of cancer. He didn't know how much longer he would live. I drove to Michigan the Saturday following our phone call. Ernie, his wife Lulu and I spent a wonderful day reminiscing at their apartment in suburban Detroit. After more than 68 years of marriage, Lulu still enjoyed sitting next to Ernie, listening, as he talked about his 55 years in broadcasting.

A few weeks later, Ernie, again, was hospitalized and there was some question as to whether or not he would survive. I called the Harwell's home phone and their number had been disconnected. I then left a message on Ernie's cell phone telling him how much I loved him and that he always would be in my thoughts. After a week had passed and I had not heard from Ernie, I did not think I ever would speak with him, again.

A few days later my telephone rang and a very upbeat and familiar voice said,

"Howard, it's Ernie Harwell! I just got out of the hospital. Thanks for your wonderful message."

I cannot put into words what hearing Ernie's voice on the phone that day meant to me. We have continued to speak several times a week. The conversations always have been upbeat. Ernie enjoys talking about the latest happenings in baseball broadcasting.

In 1952, Ernie broadcast New York Giants football games on radio with Marty Glickman. Marty, a long time New York sports broadcaster, was considered to be one of the best football and basketball announcers by his listeners. He and Ernie developed a friendship which began during that season with the Giants.

In February of 2001, I called Ernie and told him that Marty had passed away.

"Ernie," I said. "You and Marty have been two of my closest friends."

"Well, I'll try to stick around a few more years for you," Ernie replied.

Ernie, thanks for sticking around for 92 years, my friend! You always have been a man of your word. You have meant so much to so many people.

March 20, 2010

Introduction

The summer of 1961, for me, was *Camelot*. The excitement of watching Roger Maris and his Yankee teammate Mickey Mantle chase Babe Ruth's single season home run record meant everything in the world to this avid, nine-year-old, Yankees fan. The Yankees televised most of their games, so when I wasn't at Yankee Stadium with my dad, I was glued to my TV waiting to see who would hit the next homer.

Maris broke Ruth's record by belting his 61st home run on the final day of the '61 season. Roger's feat was truly inspiring. He was under enormous pressure chasing the most cherished record of the most revered figure in baseball history. I have chosen to honor Roger Maris and his "record" by writing *61* lessons. The ninth lesson is about him.

Some of the lessons are quite serious, many are there to inspire and several have tongue-in-cheek humor. All of them are about games that I have seen, people whom I have known or stories that I have been told during my many years of broadcasting baseball.

Lesson 1

Getting A "Good Jump" Can Be Meaningless

Ken Griffey, Sr. was the Indianapolis Indians Most Valuable Player in 1973. He started the 1974 season with Cincinnati and was optioned to Indianapolis in the middle of May. Six weeks later, he was recalled by the Reds and played in the Major Leagues until a neck injury, sustained in an automobile accident, forced him to retire during the 1991 season.

When you compare the Cincinnati Reds' teams of 1972 and '73, to their World Championship Clubs of 1975 and '76, you see significant changes in the outfield. The additions of Ken Griffey, Sr. and George Foster helped propel the Reds to greatness.

Ken and George played in the same outfield with the Indianapolis Indians before they were teammates with the Reds. Ken recalled one afternoon when the Indians played in Wichita, the home of the Chicago Cubs' Triple-A Farm Club.

"The sun was very strong and it was very difficult to see. I had sunglasses on and was playing right field; George was playing center field," Griffey, Sr. explained. "Pat Bourque, who was a big, strong left hand batter, hit a ball; I got a really good jump and immediately started running toward right center field. After a long run, I passed George, and saw him on the ground, laughing. I couldn't figure out what was so funny," Ken continued. "George was laughing so hard he couldn't get back on his feet. I looked around and saw Junior Kennedy, our second baseman, in the right field corner. He ran *there* to get the ball."

"Now, I was really puzzled. I had run in the opposite direction of where the ball was hit," Ken explained.

Foster, who was still laughing, said, "YOU RAN AFTER A BIRD NOT AFTER THE BALL!"

"Sunglasses weren't very good in those days," Ken said.

Lesson 2

There Are Times To Instill Confidence

Tommy John and I spent a lot of time talking baseball when Tommy broadcast the Charlotte Knights games. One of the stories he shared, illustrates the impact a manager or a coach can have on a player.

Tommy pitched for the Los Angeles Dodgers in 1976, and finished the season with a 10-10 record and a 3.09 ERA. He had missed all of the 1975 season after undergoing the elbow surgery which now bears his name.

John got off to a slow start in 1977, which also was Tommy Lasorda's first season as manager of the Dodgers. John made his third start on April 24th in Atlanta. The Dodgers got John seven runs in the first five innings. Meanwhile, the Braves "roughed up" the Dodgers lefty. The Braves hit four home runs and Lasorda lifted John from the game in the bottom of the fifth inning.

John was very upset with himself and stormed into the Dodger clubhouse. After three starts, he was 0-1 with a 9.00 ERA.

"I couldn't even go five innings to be eligible for the win," John said. "I kicked stuff around the clubhouse and made a complete fool of myself."

"Lasorda left the dugout and came into the clubhouse," John continued. "He told me to see him in his office after the game. I was wrong for the way I acted. I thought I was in big trouble. I figured Lasorda would 'air me out' and 'throw me under the bus.'"

"Shortly after the game ended, Lasorda called me into his office," John explained. "Lasorda pulled out his schedule and said, 'Tommy, you're one of my best pitchers. We're going to win this thing, and you're one of the reasons we're going to win. You will start these games (he indicated the games on the schedule). You will start every fifth day win or lose and I know you will pitch great.' *I left Lasorda's office feeling ten feet tall*," John said.

John only allowed a total of two runs in winning his next three starts He finished the season 20-7 with a 2.78 ERA and the Dodgers won the National League Pennant.

"It's not about X's and O's," John said. "It's about making people better. It's about giving people confidence."

Tommy Lasorda's ability to motivate players and instill confidence in them helped to make him a Hall of Fame Manager. Tommy John was an excellent pitcher. He rose to the occasion in big games; he was a three-time 20 game winner and finished his career with 288 victories. Many people believe he, too, belongs in the Hall of Fame.

Lesson 3

Being Nice Has Its Benefits

Jim Fregosi played in the Major Leagues for eighteen years and was a six-time All-Star. He managed in the Big Leagues for the California Angels, Chicago White Sox, Philadelphia Phillies and the Toronto Blue Jays.

Jim shared many stories from his playing days with me when he managed the Triple-A Louisville Redbirds; this one is my favorite.

One Saturday night when Jim was playing for the Angels, they were in Boston, facing the Red Sox. After the game, Jim went into a local bar and struck up a conversation with a very attractive woman.

After some small talk, Fregosi politely asked, "Would you like to leave with me?"

"Yes I would," she replied.

Jim smiled at the good news.

"And I would like you to take me to Midnight Mass!" she said, as she smiled from ear to ear.

Her words put Jim in a state of disbelief.

"Okay," he muttered. "That wasn't what I had in mind. But, if you insist on going to Midnight Mass, we'll go to Midnight Mass."

After going to Mass, the young woman drove Jim back to the hotel and the two said "good night."

The Angels and Red Sox played an afternoon game the following day. Jim came up to bat in the first inning. The first pitch thrown to him was right down the middle of the plate.

"BALL," Plate Umpire Ed Hurley called out.

Fregosi could not believe his good fortune. After all, how could Hurley not call a strike on a pitch that was right over the heart of the plate?

Jim turned to Ed Hurley and said, "Thank You, Ed."

"No," Hurley replied. "Thank you for taking MY DAUGHTER to Midnight Mass!"

Lesson 4

Given Guidance, Young Players Can Improve Dramatically

Andrew McCutchen was the Pittsburgh Pirates number one pick in the 2005 amateur draft. He rose through the Bucs' Minor League system quickly and spent the entire 2008 season with the Triple-A Indianapolis Indians. His numbers were quite respectable. He batted .283 with nine homers, 50 RBI and 34 stolen bases.

Despite those good numbers, those who watched McCutchen play on a daily basis, expressed several areas of concern:

- He was caught stealing 19 times.
- He tripled only three times in 590 at bats, even though he possessed great bat speed and great running speed.
- He rarely hit balls to the opposite field.
- He played center field and frequently was not aggressive enough in his approach to fly balls and line drives.

"Remember Andrew McCutchen is only 21 years old," Indians' Hitting Coach Hensley Meulens often said. "Be patient with him."

McCutchen made dramatic improvements in all phases of his game in 2009. He started <u>driving</u> balls to the opposite field and tripled eight times in just 219 at-bats. He only was caught stealing twice and he raised his batting average .20 points. He played a more aggressive center field and made several outstanding catches.

McCutchen played so well in Indianapolis that he was promoted to Pittsburgh on June 3rd. He was most impressive as a Pirate, too. He batted .286 with 12 homers and 54 RBI and also stole 22 bases. McCutchen finished fourth in the National League Rookie of the Year voting, despite playing in only 108 games with Pittsburgh.

What a difference one year makes!

Why the dramatic improvements?

Jeff Branson, the Indianapolis Indians hitting coach in 2009, and I spoke at length about McCutchen.

"Greg Ritchie (Pirates Hitting Coordinator) and I mapped out a plan for Andrew during Instructional League after the 2008 season," Jeff explained. "We told Andrew not to worry about pitches on the inner half of the plate. He was shortening his swing and getting far too much of his top hand involved. We told him that when he swung, he needed to keep the barrel of his bat through the strike zone, stay on the ball and lengthen the end of his swing."

"McCutchen's hands are so quick that no pitcher can 'beat' him on the inner half of the plate," Jeff continued. "Andrew began to realize this and it changed everything. He started driving balls to the opposite field; he learned pitchers' tendencies while he was batting, and also while he was running the bases. Andrew began reading 'counts' well and started to understand when to steal a base and when to stay put."

"Athletic ability and seasoning are great things," Jeff chuckled.

Lesson 5

There Are Many Roads To Cooperstown

Dallas Williams and I first were introduced when he played for the Indianapolis Indians in 1982. Dallas had put his name in the record books the previous season. One day over lunch, in 2009, we discussed his dubious claim to fame.

On Saturday, April 18, 1981, the Rochester Red Wings and Pawtucket Red Sox started the longest game in professional baseball history. The teams played 32 innings, at McCoy Stadium in Pawtucket, until the game finally was suspended the following morning at 4:07! A few months later, when the teams next met in Pawtucket, the game resumed. Pawtucket scored in the bottom half of the 33rd inning to win 3-2. Time of the game: 8 hours and 25 minutes! Two future Hall of Famers, Wade Boggs and Cal Ripken Jr., played in the game.

Dallas Williams, who had been the Orioles' number one pick in the 1976 amateur draft, was an outfielder with the Red Wings.

"We never should have played that Saturday night in April," Dallas said. "It was very cold and there was a gale blowing straight in."

Dallas failed to hit safely each time he came to bat. In the 17th inning, Dallas went into the Rochester clubhouse for a moment, where he saw outfielder Mark Corey.

"Corey had left the game several innings earlier and he had had more than a few beers," Dallas said. "I thought to myself, this is one guy who is having a rougher night than I'm having."

"The game went on and on and everyone wanted it to end except me," Dallas explained. "I wanted to keep playing until I finally got a base hit."

He never did get that base hit. Dallas finished the game **0 for 13.**

"It could have been worse," Dallas continued. "At least I was credited with two sacrifices. The official scorer didn't have to do that because each time I bunted there was one out. I could have been 0 for 15!"

The 0 for 13 is a professional baseball record for futility.

"Oh well, at least it got me a mention at the Hall of Fame," Dallas chuckled.

One man who did have a *rougher* night than Dallas was Pawtucket pitcher, Luis Aponte. Aponte drove to his apartment after play had been suspended and arrived at approximately 5 A.M. Aponte's wife refused to let him in the apartment! She did not believe his story about the game lasting 32 innings…. Aponte drove back to McCoy Stadium and returned to the clubhouse to get some sleep.

Lesson 6

Time Does Not Heal All Wounds

Larry Parrish has managed the Toledo Mud Hens since 2003. He has been generous with his time and I have learned a great deal from him.

Larry played in the Major Leagues for fifteen years and was a two-time All-Star. He hit three home runs in a game on four occasions and in 1982 he tied a Major League record by hitting three Grand Slams in a week.

Parrish became a Major Leaguer at age 19, in 1974, with the Montreal Expos. His game improved over the next five years and in 1979 he became an All-Star. Larry was off to a great start in 1980, when he was hit with a pitched ball that fractured his right wrist.

Larry saw orthopedic surgeon Dr. Frank Jobe who promptly sent Larry to a hand surgeon in California, Dr. Lis Stark. Dr. Stark's prognosis was not good.

"I could perform surgery," Dr. Stark said. "However, there are no guarantees. If you were not a professional athlete, I would not be concerned about doing the operation."

"If I were not a professional athlete, there would be no need for an operation," Larry replied.

Dr. Stark recommended that Larry give the injury time to heal since Larry did not have to pick up a bat all winter.

Parrish took Dr. Stark's advice and did not swing a bat all winter. In February, Larry reported to Spring Training at West Palm Beach. He swung a bat for the first time in months and the pain immediately returned. He was extremely frustrated, to say the least. *Time did not heal this wound.*

Larry continued to play; however, he no longer was a good hitter. The injury frustrated him to the point that he began thinking about another career.

When the Major League players went on strike in June of 1981, Larry returned to his home in Haines City, Florida. He came from a farming background and owned some cattle. Larry decided to build a new pen for his herd. He hammered away for eight hours, day after day, for approximately two months – the duration of the strike.

The strike ended in August and Larry returned to the Expos to finish out the season. He swung a bat and amazingly the pain in his right wrist was gone! *Unbelievable*!

What happened?

The consensus among the medical professionals was the constant hammering restored the blood flow to Larry's wrist. In 1981, injury rehabilitation was not nearly as sophisticated as it is today.

During the winter of 1981-82, Larry was traded to the Texas Rangers. He had several productive years with them and played in the Major Leagues through the 1988 season. He played the final two years of his career in Japan.

Lesson 7

Don't Share Your Thrills With Everyone

I was 12 years old when I attended my first World Series game. It was game three of the 1964 Fall Classic between the New York Yankees and St. Louis Cardinals. Bleacher seats at Yankee Stadium went on sale the day of the game and cost $2.00. Those same seats were priced at 75 cents during the regular season.

Curt Simmons of the Cardinals and Jim Bouton of the Yankees were the starting pitchers. The score was 1-1 going to the bottom of the ninth. Simmons had departed for a pinch-hitter in the top of the inning and Barney Schultz came on to pitch for the Cardinals.

Mickey Mantle led off for the Yankees and he belted Schultz's first pitch off the façade of the third deck in right field! The home run won the game and it gave the Yankees a two games to one lead in the Series. It was Mantle's 16th World Series homer, which broke Babe Ruth's long standing record of 15. There's no question that watching Mantle hit that home run was my greatest thrill as a youngster.

Fast forward 13 years. I was having lunch with the manager of the Indianapolis Indians, Roy Majtyka. The

Indians were in Wichita for a series with the Aeros, the Chicago Cubs Triple-A team.

A gentleman approached our table.

"Roy, how are you?" he asked.

"I'm doing fine Barney. How have you been?" Roy responded.

"I'm doing great," Barney said.

"Barney, this is Howard Kellman, our radio announcer," Roy said. "Howard, this is Barney Schultz. He used to pitch for the Cardinals."

This was not news to me.

"Barney," I said. "When you pitched for the Cardinals, you gave me the greatest thrill I ever had as a youngster."

Barney got so excited he could hardly contain himself.

"Really! When was that?" he asked.

"Game three of the 1964 World Series," I said. "Your first pitch to Mickey Mantle. He got all of it and….."

"Why you no good S..!" Barney interrupted.

With that, we all broke up laughing.

We then discussed how Barney's pitching helped the Cardinals with their great run to the National League Pennant that year. They were six and a half games behind the Philadelphia Phillies with twelve games to play. Barney recorded saves in six of the Cardinals final seven victories, including the pennant clincher on the final day of the season.

Barney Schultz also gave Cardinals fans plenty of thrills that season.

Lesson 8

Sometimes You Should Give Less Than 100%

Ron Oester was born and raised in Cincinnati and Pete Rose was his hero. Ron joined the Indianapolis Indians in 1977 and often spoke of Pete. Oester saw that Rose played with passion, at all times, so Ron always talked about *giving 110%*.

Ted Kluzewski was the Cincinnati Reds hitting coach when Sparky Anderson was the Reds skipper. After the 1978 season, the Reds assigned Kluzewski to work with Minor Leaguers. Ted had a major impact on Oester's career. One day during the 1979 season, while Ron was playing for the Indianapolis Indians (the Reds Triple-A Affiliate), Ted had a talk with him.

"Ronnie," Ted said. "You always are talking about giving 110%."

Oester eagerly nodded.

"I don't want you at 110%," Ted continued. "I don't want you giving 100% either. I would like to see you giving 95 - 98%."

Oester could not believe what he was hearing.

"Big Klu" became quite animated.

"I don't want any tension in your body when

you are hitting. 95-98% will do the job," Ted said. "When you're giving a little less than 100%, you're still aggressive, but relaxed."

Oester came to realize that Kluzewski was right on target. One of the most common mistakes in baseball is that of players *trying too hard*.

Ron Oester went on to play in the Major Leagues for more than eleven seasons. He spent his entire playing career with the Cincinnati Reds, retiring in 1990, after the Reds won the World Series.

Lesson 9

Some Potential Can Be A Very Good Thing

I smiled from ear to ear when Indianapolis Indians President Max Schumacher told me that Roger Maris had played for the Indianapolis Indians. The 1956 season with Indianapolis proved to be a very important one in Maris' career.

Roger got off to a very slow start in spring training, batting .083 in the first eight exhibition games.

"I just hope that Kerby (manager Kerby Farrell) doesn't give up on me too quickly," Roger said. "If he sticks with me, I'll start hitting. If I don't make it to Triple-A Indianapolis this year, I may never make it."

Roger began the season with Indianapolis, however; things were not going well for him or for the Indians. In those days rosters had to be trimmed one month into the season, on May 15th. Maris was *on the fence.*

Despite Maris' struggles, Farrell believed in him.

"I like this kid," Farrell said. "He has some potential."

A decision then was made that may have altered the course of baseball history. Maris remained with the Indians and in a 24-0 win over Louisville, he knocked in seven runs. That Louisville win evened Indianapolis' record at 13-13. The day proved to be the turning point for both Maris and the Tribe. Roger went on to bat .293 with 17 home runs and 75 RBI that season.

The Indians won the American Association Championship and then defeated Rochester in the Junior World Series. Roger was named the Series MVP and Kerby Farrell was named American Association Manager of the Year. Kerby may have deserved the Award simply for the confidence he showed in Maris.

Roger went on to play in the Major Leagues for twelve years. He achieved baseball immortality in 1961, when he belted 61 home runs.

Lesson 10

Your Thoughts Can Come Back To Haunt You

Don Werner spent parts of six seasons with the Indianapolis Indians (1975–1980). Don played professionally for 18 years and accumulated a little over two years of Major League service. His claim to fame was that he caught Tom Seaver's lone career no-hitter, in June of 1978.

As a youngster, Don and his dad, Bud, would make their annual three-hour drive from Appleton, Wisconsin, their hometown, to Wrigley Field, to watch the Cubs. Donnie, like so many youngsters from the Midwest in the '50's and '60's, idolized Ernie Banks. When Bud and Donnie made their visit in 1964, Donnie was especially "pumped up." During the drive to Chicago, Donnie kept thinking about Public Address Announcer Pat Piper mentioning Ernie Banks' name when Piper announced the lineups.

A few minutes before the start of the game, Piper said, "Get your scorecards and pencils ready."

Donnie was more than ready! When Piper got to the Cubs lineup, Donnie couldn't wait to shout his approval when Banks' name was announced.

"Playing first base for the Cubs, Leo Burke," Piper intoned.

Donnie could not believe his ears! He was very upset about Ernie Banks getting the day off. At age eleven, it's not surprising that much of his displeasure was directed toward Leo Burke. Although Donnie realized it was not Burke's decision to give Banks the day off, that didn't make a difference.

"Once a year I go to Wrigley Field to watch Ernie Banks play baseball and today, Leo Burke plays instead," Don said, as he shook his head in disbelief. "Leo Burke, Leo Burke, Leo Burke."

Don graduated from Appleton East High School in 1971 and was drafted in the fifth round by the Cincinnati Reds. He signed with them and rose through their farm system. He got his first taste of the Major Leagues in September of 1975.

The Reds won the National League West title by a whopping 20 games that season. The day after they clinched the West Division, Manager Sparky Anderson decided to give Johnny Bench the night off. Donnie got the nod to start behind the plate in place of Bench. As you can imagine, Donnie was pumped up! This would be his first start in the Major Leagues. He couldn't wait for Public Address Announcer Paul Sommerkamp to mention his name when the lineups and batting orders were called out. When Sommerkamp announced Donnie's name as the Reds' starting catcher, Don initially felt a tremendous sense of pride and joy. He started to go about his business, when all of a sudden he stopped dead in his tracks.

"Wait a minute," he muttered. "Wow! What if there is some kid in the stands today, who goes to a Reds game with his dad, once a year, to see Johnny Bench play? Imagine how that kid is feeling right now hearing that Johnny Bench is not playing and that Don Werner is replacing him."

"Where is Leo Burke? Where is Leo Burke? I want to apologize to him," Donnie mumbled.

Lesson 11

He Was Much More Than A Pioneer

Jackie Robinson's accomplishments in the face of adversity have been well chronicled. The support and encouragement he gave to others is not as well documented.

Former Dodgers great Carl Erskine was a broadcast partner of mine. He shared this story with me.

Before the 1948 baseball season began, the Dodgers played an exhibition game in Fort Worth, Texas against their Double-A team. Carl, who was pitching for Fort Worth, was 21 years old and pitched very well that day. Jackie Robinson made it a point to seek Carl out afterward.

"Young fellow, you're not going to be in the Minor Leagues too long, if you keep pitching like that," Jackie said.

Those words meant a great deal to Carl because they boosted his confidence. With all that Jackie Robinson experienced and endured in 1947, he still found time to encourage others.

Carl was recalled by the Dodgers during the 1948 season and began a 12 year Major League career. He threw two no-hitters, was a 20 game winner and set a World Series strikeout record. Carl and Jackie were teammates with the Dodgers for many years and became close friends.

Jackie's encouraging words were not limited to baseball players.

Jerry Harkness hit the longest shot in the history of Professional Basketball when he played for the Indiana Pacers. He has lived in Central Indiana since his playing days.

Jerry is a very quiet, pleasant man. He grew up in New York City and was so shy he did not try out for his high school basketball team. One day, in 1956, when Jerry was a junior at DeWitt Clinton High School in the Bronx, he went to the Harlem YMCA to play basketball. Jerry was shooting baskets by himself when a man who had been observing him approached.

"Young fellow, you look like a pretty good player. You can play!" the man emphatically said.

Jerry turned to look at the man and to his astonishment it was Jackie Robinson!

"Jackie Robinson thinks I'm a good player. He believes in me and my ability," Jerry whispered.

Those words from Jackie encouraged and prompted Jerry to try out for his High School team. Jerry made the team and the following year, as a senior, he led DeWitt Clinton in scoring.

Jerry received a scholarship to Loyola of Chicago and

led them to a National Championship in 1963. He then went on to play professional basketball.

We can see the importance of Jackie's words. Encouragement can be oxygen to the soul.

Lesson 12

Encouragement Has Many Faces

John Young was a career Minor Leaguer who got a "cup of coffee" (a brief call-up) with the Detroit Tigers. After his playing days were over, John had the vision to start RBI (Reviving Baseball in the Inner Cities), an organization that provides minority youth with more opportunities to play baseball.

John and I spent a lot of time talking baseball when he was a scout for the Texas Rangers and for the Florida Marlins. I have enjoyed the time I have spent with John and other scouts since most of them are wonderful people who love the game of baseball.

John made his Major League debut on September 9, 1971. In the bottom of the ninth inning, Manager Billy Martin called upon John to pinch-hit for Eddie Brinkman. John's first Major League at bat and he was facing former Cy Young award winner Jim Lonborg. John was so nervous his knees were shaking! (Every player remembers his first at bat in the Big Leagues. It is such a special moment.) John was so anxious that he swung at the first pitch and grounded out to third base. The Tigers lost the game and John was deeply disappointed.

After the game, while John was in the Tigers'

clubhouse, he was seated next to his locker. He had his head down and was rehashing his at-bat. One of the veteran players, Gates Brown, approached John and put his arm around John's shoulders. John appreciated Gates' gesture so much that he looked up and started to smile. John thought that Gates was coming over to offer some encouragement for which John was most grateful.

"Son," Gates said. "Don't feel bad. It's not your fault. You had no business being up there, anyway!"

John broke up laughing. Gates' humor lifted John's spirits and helped him relax.

John only played in one other Major League game and rapped out two hits in three at-bats. He finished his Big League career 2 for 4.

Gates Brown didn't realize he was teasing a man who would become a lifetime .500 hitter!

Lesson 13

Determination And Resiliency Are An Unbeatable Combination

Cecil Cooper managed the Indianapolis Indians during the 2003 and 2004 seasons. I found him to be a very thoughtful and considerate man and an authority on the subject of hitting. He shared the following story which illustrates why he became an excellent Major League player.

On the night of June 14, 1974, "Coop" was 24 years old and in his first full season in the Major Leagues. Cecil and the Red Sox were facing Nolan Ryan and the Angels in Anaheim. Nolan struck Cooper out in each of his first five at-bats.

Cecil's sixth time up he fouled out to Angels catcher Ellie Rodriguez. Coop received a standing ovation from the Anaheim fans because he finally had hit the ball. Cecil struck out in his next at bat and put his name in the record books. He finished the game 0 for 8. You can imagine just how horrible Cooper felt during and after the game.

Since Coop was so inexperienced, he did not have

many past successes to brighten his mood. He did have an inner strength that enabled him to bounce back. The next day he was able to rap out four base hits.

That kind of determination and resiliency paved the way for Cecil Cooper to play in the Major Leagues for fifteen years and to become a five-time All-Star.

Lesson 14

A Teacher Can Help Push You To Greatness

I had the pleasure of spending some time during the 2008 season with Hall of Famer, Paul Molitor. We met when the Indianapolis Indians were in Rochester playing the Red Wings, the Minnesota Twins' Triple-A Farm Team. These days, Paul is an instructor in the Twins' Farm system.

Tony Muser, who was one of Molitor's hitting coaches when Paul played with the Milwaukee Brewers, currently, is an instructor in the San Diego Padres' Farm system.

Tony became the Brewers hitting coach in 1987. Under Muser's tutelage, Molitor hit safely in 39 consecutive games that season. In addition to the 39 game hitting streak, Molitor raised his batting average .72 points from the previous season, to .353. Paul hit .300 or better twice in his first nine years in the Major Leagues. After Molitor and Muser started working together, Molitor batted .300 or better nine times in the next eleven years.

I spent a great deal of time with Muser during the 1991 and '92 seasons when he managed the Brewers Triple-A affiliate in Denver. Tony spoke of Molitor's dedication and Tony often would wear a t-shirt commemorating Molitor's hitting streak.

Sixteen years later, I asked Paul about his relationship with Tony.

"Tony helped me a great deal," Paul answered. "He got me out of my comfort zone. I used to try to protect my average, but with Tony constantly challenging me, I went from being a good player to playing at another level."

That *level* was "Hall of Famer."

The impact that some coaches and managers have on players can be career changing.

Lesson 15

Trouble Can Come From Strange Places

Jim McKean is a Montreal native who played in the Canadian Football League before he became an umpire. McKean was an umpiring supervisor from 2002-2009 and our paths frequently crossed. He has a pleasant disposition; however, during his days as a Major League umpire (1973-2001), he had his share of arguments with players, managers and even mascots.

One night in Arlington, Texas, the Detroit Tigers, managed by Ralph Houk, were playing the Rangers. On this particular evening, the San Diego Chicken was performing. Mascots were allowed on the field at Major League parks during games in the 1970's. Ralph Houk, a "tough guy", a Major in World War II, disdained mascots.

McKean was umpiring behind the plate and Greg Kosc was the first base umpire.

"We had a play at first base and Ralph came out to argue claiming interference should have been called," Jim said. "It was my call but I did not have a clear view of the 'interference.'" I asked Greg for help and he said that he didn't see it, either."

"I told Ralph that since neither of us saw 'interference' we would not be able to make the call," Jim continued. "Then Ralph went nuts! He started kicking dirt and throwing his hands up in the air. The Chicken started putting on a show too…. with his imitation of Ralph. The Chicken's performance and Ralph's outburst were equally entertaining to the crowd. Not only was Ralph upset with me, but he was angry at the Chicken, too. Not only was I upset with Ralph, but I was 'steaming' at the Chicken for adding fuel to the fire. It was a three way argument with everyone upset with everyone else."

"I would rather have the (bleeping) Chicken umpiring than you two (bleeping) guys!" Ralph shouted.

That did it.

"I yelled to Ralph, you're (bleeping) out of here," Jim said. "Then I turned to the Chicken and I screamed, and you're (bleeping) out of here too."

A manager and a mascot ejected on the same play!

Another time, Jim threw the Toronto Blue Jays mascot, BJ Birdie, out of a game.

"I think I had more trouble with mascots than I did with players and managers," Jim chuckled.

Lesson 16

Being Polite Does Not Always Work

Trent Jewett is a very dedicated and knowledgeable baseball man who managed the Indianapolis Indians for four years. He is well respected among umpires because he is fair and usually isn't one to hold a grudge.

On a Sunday, in late June of 2008, the Indianapolis Indians played the Columbus Clippers in Columbus. In the top half of the first inning, with a runner on third base and one out, Neil Walker was called out on strikes on a pitch that looked to be outside. Trent went out to argue and after a heated confrontation, home plate umpire R.J. Thompson, threw him out of the game. Trent seldom got ejected from games, but on this particular day, he was sent to an early shower.

The next evening, the Indianapolis Indians were at home hosting the Charlotte Knights. The same umpiring crew that had been in Columbus now was in Indianapolis.

In the sixth inning, Jewett disagreed with a check swing/strike three, call on Brian Bixler.

Trent walked over to home plate umpire Jason Klein and very politely said, "Yesterday you guys threw

me out in the top of the first. Based on what I have seen tonight, I am out here arguing on behalf of both teams."
EJECTED!

Lesson 17

Sometimes You Can't Please Anyone

People who have watched baseball for many years point out that each season they see things on the field they never have seen before. In 1999, the Indianapolis Indians and Syracuse SkyChiefs played a game in Syracuse and, to this day, I shake my head in disbelief at the strange play that I witnessed at P&C Stadium.

In the top of the seventh inning, Indianapolis' D.T. Cromer was the runner at second base when Mike Frank grounded a ball slowly to the right side. First baseman Luis Lopez fielded the ball and flipped it to pitcher Steve Sinclair, who was covering first base. First base umpire John Creek ruled that Sinclair missed the bag and called Frank safe at first. Sinclair started to argue with Creek and SkyChiefs Manager Pat Kelly bolted out of the dugout to take up the argument. Kelly was ejected by Creek within seconds after closing in on him.

Cromer had advanced from second to third on the play and then, when he saw Sinclair and Kelly arguing with Creek, Cromer dashed home. When things finally had settled down, home plate umpire Paul Emmel ordered

Cromer back to third base saying, "time had been called during the argument."

None of the Indians saw any indication of time having been called, so now it was the Indians' turn to argue. Manager Dave Miley charged out of the dugout and put on quite a show. He was quickly ejected; both managers were given an early shower on the same play! I never had seen this happen in professional baseball.

This was Miley's third ejection in the past week. I approached him in the clubhouse after the game.

"Dave, we're looking for a complete game out of you tomorrow," I said.

He smiled and chuckled and his response was unprintable.

Lesson 18

Not Everyone Wants To Be Encouraged

The Pittsburgh Pirates have been the Indianapolis Indians' parent team since 2005. This working agreement has enabled me to spend a great deal of time with Pete Vuckovich, who is a Special Assistant to Bucs General Manager, Neal Huntington. Pete's baseball knowledge is extensive and he has a unique perspective on pitching.

"Pitching is an art," Pete told me. "Home plate is the canvas, the arm is the paint brush and the ball is the paint. When you pitch, you paint a picture."

Vuckovich pitched in the Major Leagues for eleven years and won the American League Cy Young Award in 1982.

When Pete pitched for the St. Louis Cardinals, his teammate Steve Swisher, was Pete's friend and "battery" mate. (Vuckovich did not have an *early to bed, early to rise* philosophy during his playing days.) Pete and Steve went out to a bar to relax in Cincinnati the night before one of Pete's starts. At midnight, Swisher decided he wanted to return to the hotel to get some rest.

"Why are you leaving?" Pete asked. "I have to pitch tomorrow and I'm staying."

"I have to go," Swisher said, as he left for the hotel.

The next night, Pete recorded his eighth victory of that 1979 season and Swisher did not even play in the game.

"For the next four days, I was rude to Steve," Vuckovich said. "I kept reminding him that he left the bar and I stayed; and I won the game and he did not even play."

"Steve was my catcher in my next start which also was against the Reds," Pete continued. "I had nothing. The Reds were smacking balls all over the place."

Even though Pete was pitching badly, Swisher kept coming out to the mound to offer encouragement.

"Pete, you have great stuff," Steve said, on several visits. "I don't know what's happening."

In the third inning, Cardinals' Manager Ken Boyer, took Vuckovich out of the game. Pete had pitched two plus innings and allowed seven hits and eight runs.

"I went into the clubhouse and drank a bottle of beer for each half inning played," Pete admitted. "I had the empty beer bottles lined up in my locker."

Several innings after Vuckovich departed, Swisher was removed from the game, for pinch hitter, Terry Kennedy. Steve came into the clubhouse and approached Pete.

"Pete, you had great stuff. I can't figure it out. I don't know what happened out there today," Steve said.

"I don't want to hear that crap!" Pete shouted.

Pete then flung an empty beer bottle in Swisher's direction. The bottle bounced off the bottom of a nearby wall and didn't even break!

Swisher went nuts!

"I am sick and tired of lying to you!" Swisher shouted. "Now you know how horrible you were throwing today! Your stuff was so bad you couldn't even break a beer bottle!"

Both men broke up laughing. Swisher had been well intentioned with his encouraging words during the game. Steve's goal was to keep Pete's confidence up and not let a bad outing affect him. Vuckovich appreciated and understood what Swisher was trying to do; however, Pete realized how poorly he had pitched and was in no mood to listen to Swisher's kind words.

Pete's confidence never wavered. He pitched a complete game victory against the Atlanta Braves in his next start.

Lesson 19

Young Players Need Guidance

Bucky Dent and I first crossed paths when Bucky managed the Columbus Clippers in 1988. It didn't take me long to ask him about his dramatic home run for the Yankees against the Red Sox in their one game playoff in 1978.

"Had Billy Martin been our manager instead of Bob Lemon, I think I probably would have been lifted for a pinch hitter," Bucky said. (Lemon had replaced Martin as the Yankees manager in late July that season.)

"I am known for that home run. Most people forget that I was the MVP of the '78 World Series," Bucky added.

Bucky batted .417 in the Series as the Yankees defeated the Dodgers four games to two. He was a three-time All-Star, (1975, 1980, 1981) who played in the Major Leagues for 11 seasons.

"Is there anything else that people should know about your career?" I asked.

"Yes," Bucky said. "Very few people are aware of the influence Joe Sparks had upon me when I was a young player."

I knew Joe Sparks quite well from his days managing

the Indianapolis Indians. In fact, the Indians won the American Association Championship in each of Joe's three years at the helm.

"When I played in the Minor Leagues with the White Sox there were no coaches," Bucky said. "It was just the manager and the players. Joe was my manager at Class-A Appleton in 1971. I played at Double-A Knoxville in 1972 and Triple-A Iowa in 1973 and Joe managed those teams, too."

"Joe taught all of the White Sox Minor League players how to play the game the right way," Bucky added. "We were very young and he instilled confidence in us. He used his sense of humor at times; he was tough, yet fair and we all loved him."

Joe Sparks knew baseball and understood people. Over the years, there have been other notable baseball men like Joe, in the Minor Leagues. Joe is one of many who have not gotten a chance to manage in the Major Leagues. These men haven't *made it*, but I feel they should be thought of as successful because of the influence they have had on players like Bucky Dent.

Lesson 20

The *Greats* Adjust In Due Time

Gary Allenson managed the Louisville RiverBats in 1998, which is when I first met him. Allenson told me that Roger Clemens was the hardest worker Gary ever had seen in his more than 30 years in professional baseball.

"I was Roger's catcher when he made his Major League debut," Gary said. "We (Red Sox) were playing the Indians in Cleveland. It was in May of 1984."

"Clemens didn't have the split finger pitch then," Gary continued. "However, his fastball just 'jumped' at hitters. It was as if it kicked into another gear as it got close to the plate. Roger had great stuff, but did have one major challenge."

"What was that?" I asked.

"He had a very high leg kick and the Indians stole six bases against him that day," Gary said. "Even Andre Thornton stole two bases."

Clemens struggled in his debut, allowing 11 hits and 4 earned runs in 5 and 2/3 innings.

"The Boston writers approached me after the game and asked how I felt about the Indians stealing six bases against ME!" Gary emphatically said. "I decided to bite my tongue and not say anything about Roger's high leg kick and how slow he was to the plate." (Gary got a base hit that day to *raise* his average to .115. Good thing he bit his tongue.)

"Roger adjusted in due time," Gary explained to me. "He did a better job at preventing runners from stealing. He began to step off the rubber, vary his set intervals and throw over to first base more frequently."

Gary Allenson was a "good handler" of pitchers. He played in the Major Leagues for seven years. Allenson and Clemens were teammates for just one season, 1984. Gary was Clemens catcher in Roger's Big League debut but never was behind the plate for any of Clemens' 354 Major League wins.

Lesson 21

There Is More Than One Way To Make Your Point

I spent a lot of time talking baseball with Billy Connors when he was the Oklahoma City 89ers pitching coach in the late 1970's. We have stayed in touch over the years and he has shared stories from his time working with Major League players.

Billy made it to the Big Leagues as a pitching coach with the Kansas City Royals, in 1980. He also has been a pitching coach for the Chicago Cubs, Seattle Mariners and New York Yankees.

During the 1980 World Series between the Kansas City Royals and Philadelphia Phillies, Kansas City pitcher Rene Martin made his first World Series appearance in game one. Most players have some World Series "jitters" and Rene was only in his second season in the Major Leagues.

"Rene looked scared to death," Billy said. "I walked out to the mound and looked him in the eye. I told Rene that I had one thing to say to him."

Rene could barely speak.

"What's that?" he mumbled.

"I love you," Billy said.

Those three magic words! Rene smiled, relaxed and pitched well.

Fast forward two decades. Billy is a Minor League instructor with the New York Yankees. He introduces himself to Roger Clemens.

"Roger," Billy said. "I'm Billy Connors, and I have been a Major League pitching coach for many years. May I say something to you?"

"Yeah, sure," Roger replied.

"You're horse s….!" Billy said.

Roger looked stunned.

"You're just nibbling and not going after hitters. When you were successful, you pitched much more aggressively," Billy explained.

That was exactly what Roger needed to hear. His pitching improved.

Good coaches and good managers have the knack of saying the right thing at the right time.

Lesson 22

Games Can Be Cancelled For Many Reasons

Sal Butera caught for the Indianapolis Indians in 1984. He first made it to the Major Leagues in 1980, after spending eight years in the Minor Leagues. These days, he is a Special Assistant to General Manager, Alex Anthopoulos, with the Toronto Blue Jays.

When Sal and I speak, he often tells stories from his playing days. One that I never will forget took place when he played for Triple-A Tacoma, in the Pacific Coast League.

"We were playing Spokane in the last series of the season and had had three straight rainouts," Butera explained. "The field was an absolute disaster. However, our General Manager, Stan Naccarato, scheduled a day-night doubleheader to try to recoup some of the money lost from the postponements."

"That morning, management did its best to dry out the field," Sal continued. "The first thing they tried was to have an army helicopter hover twenty feet above ground. When the helicopter didn't dry the field, the grounds crew poured gasoline along the foul lines and home plate area. They set the gasoline on fire and eventually the fire burned itself out. Finally, the field was dry enough to start the game."

"We began to play and I was catching. The second batter came to the plate and while I couldn't see that anything was wrong, I began to feel lightheaded," Sal added. "Eric Gregg was the plate umpire and after two more pitches Eric collapsed right on top of me. Eric had passed out and a moment later everyone left the field."

This may have been the only time in baseball history that a game was called due to *gas fumes*.

Lesson 23

Shared Knowledge Can Bring Success

Brian Dorsett played for the Indianapolis Indians and today he is a successful entrepreneur in Terre Haute, Indiana. Brian also has done color commentary on televised Indianapolis Indians games for several years.

Dorsett had his share of serious injuries during his playing days. In 1987, elbow problems and an operation to repair the damage robbed him of arm strength. By 1994, he had had six arthroscopic surgeries on his right knee. Brian did not want to miss a full year of action so he never had the knee surgically reconstructed. The surgeries left Brian with no range of motion in his knee; he had to assume his crouch while he was leaning on his left side.

"I never told anyone how much my knee hurt," Dorsett said, while he reflected on his career. "I took my share of Advil, that's for sure. I was able to accumulate some Major League time with the Indians, Yankees, Padres, Reds and Cubs."

"The only year of my career that I didn't spend any time in the Minor Leagues was 1994," Brian continued. "It also was the first time I had a former Gold Glove catcher as my instructor. Bob Boone's advice helped my throwing a great deal, yet he never knew how much my knee hurt."

"Bob helped me with the exchange from my glove to my throwing hand," Brian emphasized. "His advice helped me compensate for my knee injury and my lack of arm strength. Bob explained that I should receive the ball deeper with my throwing hand behind my glove, so that my glove and throwing hand were closer to my body. This change enabled me to have a much quicker transfer from my glove to my throwing hand. I didn't have to go out to get the ball as I had been doing."

"I only wish I had met Bob Boone sooner," Brian said.

Lesson 24

Some People Talk Yet Never Say Anything

Scott Service pitched for the Indianapolis Indians for seven consecutive seasons. His teammates gave him the nickname, "The Big Dummy." Try to decide if this nickname was appropriate.

Scott Service was likeable and friendly, but since he talked incessantly he could get on people's nerves. He never stopped talking yet seldom said anything of substance.

"Are you local or are you from around here?" Service asked every bus driver.

After one of Service's brilliant monologues, teammate Scott Ruskin chimed in.

"Hey Servy, that's great deductive reasoning," Ruskin said.

For the next three hours, Service pleaded with Ruskin to explain what Ruskin meant by his "deductive reasoning" comment.

In 1997, Service was the Indians' closer. He was having an excellent season, but then hit a "rough stretch." During this challenging time, he didn't slow down verbally.

At the airport, one morning, I was the target of his

words, none of which contained more than one syllable. Finally, I had had enough.

"Scott," I said. "You are full of B.S. ….Blown Saves!"

My words quieted him for about five seconds.

One night late in the 1991 season, the Indians were playing in Omaha. After the game, Service found out that his contract had been sold to the Chunichi Dragons. Scott was very excited about playing baseball in Japan. He was going to be making much more money than he was making at the Triple-A level.

When I congratulated him on his move, he could not contain his joy.

"Howard," he exclaimed. "I am 6 foot 6 inches tall. Many of the Japanese people are so much shorter. This is going to be *just* like going to a foreign country!"

I never accused him of being inaccurate.

Lesson 25

Christopher Columbus Discovered More Than America

In the late 1980's, the Indianapolis Indians had a hard throwing right handed pitcher named Mike Smith. He had a blazing fastball and a knee buckling curve. However, he never had much success at the Major League level. There is a lot more to being a good pitcher than having a great arm.

Smith was a likeable guy who was known for his *Smittyisms.*

When Mike checked out of the Ramada Inn in Omaha, he told the clerk at the front desk he was there to pay his *accidentals*. He once asked a waitress to put some *neutrons* on his salad. When Mike was asked what his girlfriend did for a living, he replied, "She's a *pseudo-pharmacologist.*"

After the Indians had played the last game of a road trip in Louisville, Mike was asked if he was returning to Indianapolis on the team bus or by car.

"I am going to take the bus," he replied. "It has bigger wheels than a car so it should get to Indy faster."

Mike had a great sense of history. He and teammate Razor Shines were having lunch one day in Buffalo, when Mike spotted a picture on the wall.

"Is that a picture of Christopher Columbus?" Mike asked.

"Yes it is," Razor replied.

"I know Christopher Columbus discovered America," Mike said. "Did Columbus discover Buffalo, too?"

Lesson 26

Be Careful – You Never Know With Whom You Are Speaking

Hall of Famer Joe "Ducky" Medwick is the last National Leaguer to win Baseball's Triple Crown. He accomplished the feat with the St. Louis Cardinals in 1937.

I spent some time with him when he was the Cardinals' Minor League Hitting Instructor. The first time we met was in Tulsa, when the Indianapolis Indians were playing the Tulsa Oilers, the Cardinals' Triple-A Farm Team.

"Joe, my name is Howard Kellman. I broadcast the Indianapolis Indians games," I said.

"Hey kid, do you know much about me," he replied.

I rattled off his accomplishments and then added that I knew that he was a "tough guy."

"I didn't take any s…. from anybody," he declared. "I will tell you a story to show you what I mean. We (Cardinals) were playing the Cubs at Wrigley Field; I hit a ball off the wall in right center field, and I was thinking triple. The throw to the Cubs third baseman Stan Hack was in plenty of time. However, when I slid I kicked the ball loose and my spikes cut Stan on the left arm. I was safe," Medwick explained.

"The Cub fans went crazy," Medwick continued. "They were screaming at me for several minutes and as things were quieting down, this one fan in the third base stands continued screaming at me at the top of his lungs. I was yelling at him too."

Stan Hack got involved even though he was upset with Medwick.

"Joe, do you know who that is? Do you know who you are yelling at?" Stan asked.

"I don't give a s…. who it is," Medwick responded.

After Hack persisted, Medwick finally relented.

"Okay, who is this guy that I am yelling at, the one that's screaming at me?" Medwick questioned.

"JOE, THAT'S AL CAPONE!" Hack shouted.

"I was shocked! At that point, I stopped yelling at him," Medwick said. "After the game, back at the hotel, I bolted the door and stacked all of the furniture against it."

Medwick did not get much sleep that night and learned a very valuable lesson.

Lesson 27

Intra-squad Games Can Have Incredible Ramifications

In 1963, the Chicago White Sox were the Indianapolis Indians' parent team. That year, the White Sox had three promising young pitchers and they decided they were going to keep two of them. They were set on keeping Dave DeBusschere and had to make a decision as to whether they would protect Denny McLain or Bruce Howard. It was a difficult choice to make. The White Sox decided to let McLain and Howard oppose one another in an intra-squad game to assist in the decision making. All of the Sox "top brass" were on hand and although McLain pitched well, Howard was the better pitcher that day.

The White Sox protected Howard and the Detroit Tigers claimed McLain on waivers. McLain went on to win 31 games and a Cy Young Award in 1968. He and Mike Cuellar shared the Cy Young Award in 1969.

Unfortunately for the White Sox, Dave DeBusschere gave up baseball after the 1965 season to devote all of his energy to basketball. DeBusschere went on to become a Hall of Fame basketball player. Bruce Howard did not distinguish himself in his Major League career.

In baseball, it is very difficult to project whether or not

young players will reach their full potential. Throughout baseball history there are stories similar to this one. However, in the last 75 years, only one pitcher has won as many as 30 games in a season: Denny McLain.

Lesson 28

When Pitch Comes To Shove, Humor Is The Answer

John "Champ" Summers and Doug Capilla were very intense players and teammates on the 1978 Indianapolis Indians. Summers had a magnificent season; he batted .368 with 34 Home Runs and 124 RBI and was named Minor League Player of the Year. Capilla, a pitcher, started the '78 campaign with Cincinnati. After struggling with the Reds, he was optioned to Indianapolis where he went 10-6 with a 5.45 ERA.

Summers was given the nickname "Champ" as a child, by his father, who had been a boxer while he was in the Navy. Like his father, Champ served in the military. He was in the Army and served in Vietnam during the Tet Offensive. Champ didn't sign a contract to play pro-ball until age 25. When Summers played for Oakland in 1974, Reggie Jackson encouraged him to go by "Champ."

Capilla was born in Honolulu. He was a left hander who had "good stuff." Doug spent parts of six seasons in the Major Leagues. He never was able to consistently throw strikes and saw his last Big League time at age 29.

Summers was 6'2" and weighed 205 pounds. He was very strong and had a short fuse. Capilla was 5'8" and checked in at 175 pounds. He was so tightly wound that in a brawl with the Denver Bears, Capilla literally charged at four of the Bears' players.

One particularly steamy summer evening in Evansville, the Indianapolis Indians and Evansville Triplets were getting set to play. (If you ever go to Evansville in the summer, bring plenty of air conditioning with you.) I was sitting in the dugout chatting with several Indians' players when along came Doug Capilla. Capilla started giving his opinions on just about everything, including Dodger Stadium.

"The ball carries well at Dodger Stadium," Capilla said.

BINGO! Summers "lost it."

"You're crazy," Summers said. "The ball **does not** carry well at Dodger Stadium!"

Capilla then yelled, "The ball **very well** at Dodger Stadium!"

Summers came right back at Capilla and started screaming at him.

"You don't know what you're talking about!" Summers shouted.

The yelling continued for another moment or so. I feared they were about to come to blows. To be more specific, I thought Summers was going to do so much damage to Capilla, that someone might have to post bail for Champ.

Capilla, shouted louder than ever, "THE BALL DOES CARRY VERY WELL AT DODGER STADIUM!"

Summers responded by shouting even louder than Capilla had shouted, "THE ONLY TIME THE BALL *EVER* CARRIES WELL AT DODGER STADIUM IS WHEN <u>YOU'RE</u> PITCHING!"

Everyone broke up laughing and an extremely tense situation was defused. One thing about Champ, he did have a sense of humor.

Lesson 29

The Great Ones Will Even The Score

Paul "Dizzy" Trout pitched in the Major Leagues for fourteen seasons. He won twenty games for the Detroit Tigers in 1943 and twenty-seven more in 1944.

Dizzy's younger brother, Don, and I were friends until Don's death in 2007. Don owned a car dealership in Lafayette, Indiana and he often would tell me stories about Dizzy.

Shortly after Dizzy made it to the Major Leagues with the Tigers, he faced the great Ted Williams. Dizzy rose to the occasion and struck Ted out. Ted rarely fanned so Dizzy was feeling mighty good about himself. He felt so good that he went into the Red Sox clubhouse after the game and asked Ted to autograph the ball! Ted was *stunned* at the request and glared at Dizzy. A moment later, Ted signed the ball.

Dizzy pitched against Ted a few weeks later and Ted belted a monstrous home run. Dizzy was shocked by how far the ball traveled.

To make matters worse, after Ted rounded second base he shouted to Dizzy,

"Hey Kid! Go get that ball and I will autograph IT too!"

Lesson 30

It Takes Time To Become A "Big Unit"

Over the years, there have been more stories about pitchers who threw extremely hard but could not consistently find the strike zone, than there have been of pitchers like Sandy Koufax and Randy Johnson, who achieved elite status after harnessing their control.

Randy Johnson pitched for the Indianapolis Indians in 1988 and struggled during the early stages of that season. He threw very hard and was quite intense, but because his control wasn't good, it was difficult to predict what the future held for him.

Randy had a strong working relationship with the Indians pitching coach, Joe Kerrigan. At the time, Joe pointed out that due to Randy's height (6'10"), there might be some challenges with his mechanics.

I could see how competitive Johnson was when I watched him pitch for the Indians; however, at that time he did not always channel his fire in the right direction. Randy became angry one night and punched a bat rack and broke a bone in his right hand. His actions were most unfortunate, but Randy did have the presence of mind to hit the bat rack with his non-throwing hand.

When the injury healed and Johnson was ready to pitch again, the Expos (Indianapolis' parent team) wanted Johnson to pitch in a simulated game. This presented quite a problem. Randy threw very hard and didn't have good control; therefore none of his teammates, with the exception of Razor Shines, would agree to bat against him.

Indians staffers came up with an idea to remedy the problem…. Bruce Schumacher, the Indians Ticket Manager, went to the Children's Museum of Indianapolis to borrow a mannequin which would be used to simulate a batter standing at the plate. Randy left his mark on the mannequin by denting it….good thing it was a mannequin and not a player.

Kerrigan spent a considerable amount of time working with Johnson on his delivery. Johnson made great strides during the season and earned a September call-up to Montreal. The Expos traded Randy to Seattle early in the 1989 season. He pitched for the Mariners for several years and continued to improve.

Toward the end of the 1992 season, Randy Johnson had the opportunity to speak with Nolan Ryan, who was still pitching for the Texas Rangers. Nolan made a suggestion to Randy that turned out to be career-changing. Ryan studied Johnson's delivery and advised him to land on the *ball* not the *heel* of his *front* foot.

Johnson made the change; his control dramatically improved and he went from being a good pitcher to being a *great* pitcher. The improvement in his control coupled with his great determination to succeed, made him unstoppable. Randy won five Cy Young Awards and over 300 games in his career.

Indianapolis Indians fans can say with pride that they had the opportunity to watch Randy when he was a young pitching prospect. They were able to follow his transformation from being a raw talent to a sensational pitcher.

We look forward to the day Randy "The Big Unit" Johnson is inducted into Baseball's Hall of Fame.

Lesson 31

You Had Better Be Thorough

If you watch a lot of baseball, there will be times when you will be uncertain about something that is happening on the field. That was the case when I was broadcasting an Indianapolis Indians – Denver Zephyrs game in the Mile High City in 1984.

Denver manager, Vern Law, went out to the mound to make a pitching change. He wanted left hander Guy Hoffman to come into the game. Hoffman got to the mound, but before he began taking his warm-up tosses he walked off the mound and into the dugout.

I wondered whether there was some kind of injury; however, Hoffman never threw a warm-up pitch and was not favoring either leg when he walked to the dugout. Finally, word came from the press box clarifying the situation. Vern had forgotten to list several of his relief pitchers on the line-up card that he had given to the umpires before the game. Players not listed on the line-up card were not allowed to play.

Anyone can make a mistake. Therefore, the reaction to this incident might have been to overlook it. However, this was not the first time that Vern omitted his pitchers from the line-up card. It was the last time, though. Vern was fired the next day.

Vern Law was a very fine pitcher who won the Cy Young Award in 1960. Success as a player does not necessarily translate into success as a manager.

Lesson 32

If You Are Going To Do Something, Make Note Of It

Charlie Leibrandt spent the 1981 and '83 seasons pitching for Triple-A Indianapolis and 1980 and '82 hurling for the Cincinnati Reds. His career was at a standstill in 1983 while he was with the Indians.

In 1982, Bob Tufts, pitched for the Triple-A Omaha Royals and had a great year. He was 10-6 with a 1.60 ERA. Tufts was a sinker/slider pitcher who did not throw very hard. A lefty like Leibrandt, Tufts, also, was not doing especially well in 1983. They were traded for one another on June 7th.

A few days after the Tufts - Leibrandt trade was made, Indianapolis' manager Roy Hartsfield and I were speaking in Roy's office.

"I forgot to do something I was going to do," Roy said.

"What's that?" I asked.

"I meant to include in my report about the Omaha Royals that Bob Tufts was not throwing the ball well this season," Roy replied. "The Reds might not have made the trade if they had known he was pitching poorly."

Tufts continued to struggle with the Indianapolis

Indians. He finished 2-3 with two saves and a 6.43 ERA. Tufts retired after that season since no team had an interest in signing him.

Charlie Leibrandt spent the remainder of the 1983 season and the beginning of the '84 campaign in Omaha. He started pitching more aggressively, and cut down the on the number of walks he issued. The lefty righted himself and went on to win 17 games for the 1985 World Champion Kansas City Royals. He continued to be a good Major League pitcher for the next ten years, winning 124 games after the trade.

What a lesson for all of us. If you are going to do something, make note of it, so as not to forget it.

Lesson 33

There Are Different Kinds Of Pressure

I enjoy spending time with former Indianapolis Indian Joe Altobelli, whenever the Indians play in Rochester. Altobelli, "Mr. Baseball" in Rochester, is a former Rochester Red Wings player, manager, broadcaster and General Manager.

There is an expression that says, "Don't be the successor. Be the successor to the successor." Altobelli was the "successor" when he was hired to manage the Baltimore Orioles prior to the 1983 season. Earl Weaver, who had just retired, had managed the Orioles for almost *15 years*. During Weaver's tenure the Orioles won six Divisional Titles, four Pennants and a World Championship, assuring him of an induction into Baseball's Hall of Fame.

I asked Joe about the pressure of succeeding Weaver.

"Pressure is just a word," Joe said. "Pressure should be part of something good. I knew all of the coaches and several of the players that I would be managing, since I had managed in the Orioles' Minor League system. My only disappointment was that Bobby Grich and Don Baylor no longer were there. I managed them in the Minor Leagues and they were like sons to me."

"Managing is a tough job, but I was thankful that I wasn't working in a factory," Joe continued.

The Orioles won the American League East that season. Their opponent in the League Championship Series was the Chicago White Sox. The "LCS" was a best-of-five in those days. The fourth game was scoreless until the tenth inning when Tito Landrum homered for Baltimore. That homer was enough for the Orioles to capture the American League Pennant.

Did Joe feel pressure during that particular game?

"I wouldn't call it pressure," Joe said. "However, my whole life flashed in front of me. Everything was in slow motion. I thought of my father taking me to games when I was a kid in Detroit…. With all of that running through my mind, I still never stopped managing."

Joe Altobelli's Orioles brought the World Championship to Baltimore by defeating the Phillies in the World Series.

"I am 77 years old now and I do feel pressure these days just trying to get out of bed in the morning," he chuckled.

Lesson 34

Never Mess With Your Manager

Each team has its share of "challenging" moments during the course of a long baseball season. In June of 1966, when the Indianapolis Indians were struggling, General Manager Max Schumacher and Manager Les Moss thought that the players needed to "loosen up" a bit. Their plan was to let the players have some drinks on their charter flight from Denver to Oklahoma City.

Many of the players took advantage of the offer. After a few drinks, outfielder Bill Voss started feeling a "little too good." Voss, who was quite thin, challenged the much stronger Moss to an arm wrestle. Les declined Bill's offer, but Bill was very persistent. Unfortunately, Moss agreed to arm wrestle Voss. It did not take Les long to pin Bill and in so doing Les broke one of Bill's fingers!

How was Les Moss going to explain this one?

Les told the Chicago White Sox (Indianapolis' parent team) and the Indianapolis newspapers that Bill Voss had broken his finger on a rundown play.

Max, Les and Bill felt awful about what had happened on the plane. Les, also, did not feel good about lying to his boss, C.V. Davis, who was the White Sox Assistant Farm Director.

Some 30 years later, when C.V. Davis was in Indianapolis on a scouting trip, and working for a different organization, Max told C.V. the truth about the incident. Since so much time had passed, both men were able to laugh and see the humor in the situation.

There are several lessons here. If only the Indianapolis Indians had been playing better, we would not have had to learn any of them.

Lesson 35

Don't Take Anything For Granted

On a June evening in Nashville, in 1986, the Nashville Sounds were playing host to the Indianapolis Indians. The Sounds were coming off of a couple of very difficult extra inning losses. Before the game, their manager, Leon Roberts, told me that his team had been playing well, but was having some *tough luck*.

On this night, the Sounds held a 9-1 lead in the seventh inning. Roberts decided that he no longer would coach third base since the Sounds had what appeared to be an insurmountable lead. He assigned those responsibilities to his hitting coach, Gene Roof.

The Sounds had men on first and second with two outs and there was a base hit. Now, Gene Roof had to make a decision. On one hand, he may not have wanted to *rub it in* by waving the man in from second to score. On the other hand, if the runner EASILY could have scored on the hit (which was the case here), most baseball people would say he should have been sent home, so the batter could have been credited with an RBI.

To this day, I still can see Gene Roof holding the

runner at third base. The next batter was retired so the runner at third did not score.

Guess what happened?

Indianapolis rallied for three runs in the eighth inning and five more in the ninth to tie the game. The Indians then scored again in the tenth inning to pull off an incredible come from behind win. Yes, a great win for Indianapolis and a devastating loss for Nashville.

It's always interesting to see how a manager reacts when his team loses a very big lead late in the game.

I spoke with Leon Roberts in the Sounds' clubhouse the next day.

"Remember what I told you yesterday," Roberts said. "We just can't seem to win these extra inning games."

He's right, isn't he?

Lesson 36

Bosses Can Be Outsmarted

Gene Tenace came into the National spotlight in 1972, when he was the World Series Most Valuable Player. Gene belted four home runs in the Series as the Oakland A's defeated the Cincinnati Reds in seven games.

Gene was a coach with the Toronto Blue Jays in 2009. We chatted when the Blue Jays were in Detroit. Gene told me about a contract disagreement he had with A's owner Charlie Finley.

"I wanted $38,000 and Finley didn't want to give it to me. This was before free agency, so I didn't have much leverage," Gene said. "Charlie ran the team from his home in Northwest Indiana and he called me when he flew to Oakland. It was a rainy day and he pulled me off the racquetball court."

"Meet me at the Edgewater Hyatt Hotel," Charlie said.

"Okay," Gene answered.

Finley always had his secretary, Carolyn, with him whenever he had a business meeting. Charlie, Carolyn and Gene sat down at a table at the hotel restaurant.

"Sign this contract," Finley demanded.

"No, I won't sign it," Gene said. "I want $38,000 and

this contract is for $35,000. A moment later, Charlie had to excuse himself because he received a long distance phone call. Carolyn and I started to speak about my contract."

"I would like to see you get the $38,000," she said. "I have an idea."

"What is it?" Gene asked.

"Do you have a dog?" she questioned.

"Yes," Gene answered.

"Gene, you know that Charlie likes creative ideas. Why don't you tell him you will accept his offer of $35,000, if he agrees to throw in a year's supply of dog food," Carolyn said.

"I'll try it," Gene replied.

Finley returned to the table a few minutes later.

"Charlie," Gene said. "I will accept your offer of $35,000 with one condition."

"What's that?" Finley asked.

"You throw in a year's supply of dog food," Gene said.

Finley thought about the proposition for a moment.

"I like that idea," Charlie said, with a smile.

Charlie pulled out the contract for $35,000 and wrote on it that he would pay for a year's supply of dog food. He started to hand the contract to Gene to sign and then Charlie abruptly stopped.

"What kind of dog do you have?" Finley asked.

"A 150 pound St. Bernard," Gene said, with an ear to ear grin.

"You no good S..!" Finley shouted. "Here's your contract for $38,000."

Lesson 37

Some Nicknames Are Well Earned

Allen Levrault pitched for the Indianapolis Indians in 2000 and 2001. I introduced myself to him when he joined the ballclub.

"Allen, I'm Howard Kellman, broadcaster for the team," I said.

"Don't call me Allen," he replied. "Call me *Meat* (short for Meathead). "Everyone calls me *Meat*."

"I'm sorry," I replied. "I did not mean to offend you."

"It's okay," he said. "But don't do it again."

A few weeks into the 2000 season Allen approached me.

"Do you know any car dealers in Indianapolis?" he asked.

"Yes," I replied.

"I am looking for a car," he said. "It doesn't have to be great, but I want it to be reliable, with good gas mileage, in pretty good shape and not too small."

"I understand," I said. "Approximately how much money do you want to spend?"

"About two hundred dollars," he replied. (He was completely serious.)

During the 2000 season, Allen was recalled by the Milwaukee Brewers, Indianapolis' parent team. The Brewers were in Minnesota to play the Twins. After some travel challenges, Allen arrived at the Metrodome. Within a half hour of his arrival, he realized he had left his baseball bag in the taxicab. The clubhouse attendants tried to track the bag down. Finally, they received a call from the cab company dispatcher saying they had found a baseball bag.

"I don't think the bag belongs to Allen Levrault," the dispatcher said.

"Why do you say that?" one of the clubhouse attendants responded.

"It doesn't have his name on the bag," the dispatcher pointed out.

"Well, what does it say on the bag?" the clubby asked.

"Meat," the dispatcher replied.

Lesson 38

Exhibition Games Are Very Important To Some People

The Indianapolis Indians have played in a beautiful downtown ballpark, Victory Field, since 1996. Attendance records recently have been set, not only in Indianapolis, but throughout the Minor Leagues with the influx of new stadiums.

I occasionally reminisce with Indians executives Cal Burleson and Randy Lewandowski about the old days at Bush Stadium when crowds were small. In fact, when Cal and I started working for the Tribe in the mid 1970's, average attendance was less than 2,000 fans per game.

June 20, 1974 was a special day for the Indianapolis Indians franchise. The Indians' parent team, the Cincinnati Reds, came to Indianapolis for their annual exhibition game. The large crowd expected for the game with the Reds was the difference between the Indians finishing the season a good deal in the "red" or slightly in the "black." In fact, Indians Manager Vern Rapp told me, the only time I would see General Manager Max Schumacher nervous, would be if it rained the day of the Reds game. If the game were to get rained out, it would not have been rescheduled and the "gate" would have been lost.

Sure enough, it rained lightly most of the day, but the game started on time. Five blocks from Bush Stadium, it poured while the game was in progress. However, it did not rain heavily at the ballpark and the game was played in its entirety.

The fans attending the game were happy for several reasons:
- Most of the Cincinnati Reds' stars played
- The Indianapolis Indians won the game
- Johnny Bench hit a home run

Max Schumacher was elated that the game was not rained out.

"Being able to play that game makes up for all the bad luck I ever have had in my life," Max said.

Indians' catcher Sonny Ruberto approached me in the clubhouse after the game.

"What did you think of Johnny Bench hitting that home run?" Sonny asked.

"I thought it was great," I answered. "That's exactly what the fans came to see."

"I agree with you completely," Sonny replied. "Everyone in the ballpark except (Indians pitcher) Pat Zachry was happy about Bench's homer. And…Zach doesn't know and doesn't need to know that when I called for the fastball, I told Johnny a fastball was coming!"

Lesson 39

You Can't Win Some Arguments

Nothing upsets managers more than when players run the bases poorly. Mistakes on the bases can cost a team several games during the course of a season. Unfortunately, some players think they should try to steal bases no matter what the situation is in the game.

Steve Hecht played for the Indianapolis Indians in 1991. He had great speed and was a good base stealer.

One night, Indianapolis was trailing by five runs and there were two men out in the eighth inning. Hecht was on second base and there was a left hand batter at the plate. DOWN BY FIVE RUNS, TWO MEN OUT AND A LEFT HAND BATTER AT THE PLATE IN THE 8TH INNING! BINGO! Hecht tried to steal third base and was thrown out.

When Steve and I spoke in the clubhouse, the next day, he told me that he had received a lot of criticism for attempting to steal in that situation.

Steve shot down his critics and said, "Howard, if I had made it, everyone would have said it was a great play!"

Good thing I wasn't on the air at the moment. His logic left me speechless.

Lesson 40

Radar Guns Can Be Overrated

I had the good fortune of interviewing Hall of Famer Whitey Ford during the 1998 season. It was an especially pleasurable assignment, since he was my favorite pitcher as a youngster.

I was reminded of Whitey, when I watched Tommy John pitch because their "deliveries" were so similar. In addition, neither man was a power pitcher.

When I discussed the subject of *radar guns* and the *art of pitching* with both men, on separate occasions, each said the same thing to me virtually word for word.

"If they had those '*things*' years ago, no team would have signed me," each man emphasized. Those "*things*" are radar guns. I found it quite interesting that both Tommy and Whitey substituted the word "*things*" for radar guns.

These days most ballparks have radar guns. It's fun for the fans to see how hard a pitcher is throwing, however, many pitchers and scouts get overly concerned about those readings.

I am convinced that there is a correlation between all of the "Tommy John" surgeries being performed and all of the emphasis on velocity. In addition to velocity, pitching involves movement and control. Even before radar guns became prominent, former Major League manager Birdie Tebbetts used to say, "Don't tell me how hard a man throws, tell me if he can pitch!"

A pitchers goal should be to get hitters out. Period!

As Hall of Fame manager Joe McCarthy said many decades ago in his "Ten Commandments of Baseball," "A pitcher who hasn't control hasn't anything."

Whitey Ford and Tommy John had GREAT CONTROL.

Lesson 41

Attitude Is The Most Important Word In The English Language

There was plenty of excitement in Cincinnati on the final day of the 1964 season. The Reds were hosting the Philadelphia Phillies at Crosley Field. The Reds and St. Louis Cardinals were tied for first place in the National League and the Phillies were just a game out of first.

Joe Nuxhall and Gordy Coleman played for the Reds that year. Both Joe and Gordy worked for the Reds in their post-playing days; Joe as a broadcaster and Gordy in the front office. When Cincinnati was the Indianapolis Indians' parent team, I spent a great deal of time talking with both men.

One day, I brought up the subject of that 1964 pennant race. The disappointment on both of their faces became quite apparent. Joe and Gordy explained that Reds Manager Dick Sisler could have pitched Jim Maloney, on three days rest, on the season's final day. Maloney had pitched eleven scoreless innings in his previous start, so Sisler opted to pitch John Tsitouris.

I was stunned at the next thing Gordy told me.

"Tsitouris came to the ballpark with all of his

belongings packed and ready to go to his home in South Carolina," Gordy lamented.

If the Reds had won, they either would have won the pennant or they would have had a one game playoff with the Cardinals to determine the pennant winner. **And…. their starting pitcher came to the ballpark prepared to go to his winter home!** (John Tsitouris certainly was not a follower of Dr. Norman Vincent Peale and the teachings in his book, The Power of Positive Thinking.)

"We (Reds players) couldn't believe what we were seeing," Gordy said.

Do I have to tell you what happened?

The Phillies scored three runs in the third inning and knocked Tsitouris out of the box. Philadelphia went on to blank the Reds, 10-0. The Cardinals won their game against the Mets to capture the National League Pennant, and yes, John Tsitouris was off to South Carolina.

Henry Ford was right when he said, "Whether you think you can or whether you think you can't, you're right."

Lesson 42

Don't Saddle Yourself With Limitations

I remembered the name Tom Walker from his days as a Major League pitcher in the 1970's. Tom and I connected during the 2008 season when his son, Neil, played third base for the Indianapolis Indians.

Tom enjoys talking about his years in professional baseball and is most proud of something he accomplished while he was pitching in the Minor Leagues.

On August 4, 1971, Tom was the starting pitcher for the visiting Double-A Dallas-Fort Worth Spurs in their game, in Albuquerque, against the Dukes. There was some doubt as to whether or not the game would be played since it had rained in the early evening.

The game did start on time and Tom pitched inning after inning without allowing a hit. He threw a 93 mph fastball, a slider and a change-up. (In those days, nobody was overly concerned about pitch counts, which is why Tom continued to pitch.)

In the top of the 15th inning (YES, THE 15th INNING!), the Spurs Manager Cal Ripken, Sr., approached Tom. Ripken, Sr., made it quite clear to Tom that the bottom of the 15th would be his last inning. It just so happened that the Spurs' Enos Cabell doubled in the game's first run as Walker and Ripken, Sr., spoke.

Tom pitched hitless ball in the bottom of the 15th. A 15 INNING NO-HITTER!

Tom said that he was physically and mentally drained after the game. His teammate, Dyar Miller, told me that there were very few "hard hit" balls against Tom that evening. Dyar said that everyone in the Spurs' dugout was amazed that Tom kept going out there each inning.

Did Tom get a promotion? That question can be best answered by taking note of this: only once in the last 89 years has a Major League team had four 20 game winners in the same season - the 1971 Baltimore Orioles, the Spurs' parent team. Jim Palmer, Dave McNally, Mike Cuellar and Pat Dobson accomplished the feat.

Tom stayed with the Dallas-Fort Worth Spurs for the remainder of the '71 season.

The no-hitter turned out to be *the turning point* in his career. He was rewarded that winter when the Montreal Expos selected him in the Rule V draft. Tom then pitched in the Major Leagues for the next six years.

Lesson 43

Don't Make Promises You Don't Intend To Keep

Joaquin Andujar pitched for the Indianapolis Indians in 1974, before embarking on a successful thirteen year career in the Major Leagues. Joaquin sometimes had difficulty controlling his emotions; however he had a good heart and many people who knew him well, liked him a great deal.

"I am one tough Dominican," Joaquin often would say.

He was not a fighter, although he "talked a pretty good game."

Ken Oberkfell and Andujar were teammates with the St Louis Cardinals. Oberkfell managed the Buffalo Bisons in 2009 and shared the following story about Joaquin with me.

George Hendrick was the Cardinals' big RBI man in the early 1980's. Chicago Cubs pitchers often would throw at Hendrick and hit him with pitched balls. This upset the Cardinals and Joaquin decided he was going to retaliate.

Andujar approached Hendrick and Oberkfell and was quite animated.

"I am going to drill (Cubs catcher) Jody Davis!" Joaquin shouted.

"Great!" said Hendrick. "Ken and I will play in at third and first base. If Davis charges the mound, we will get him before he can reach you."

When Jody Davis came up to bat Oberkfell and Hendrick were ready. It was well known that Davis was a very slow runner who never bunted, so everyone except Joaquin was perplexed that Oberkfell and Hendrick were *playing in* at third and first. They were set to run toward the front of the mound to protect Andujar. The chance of Davis being angry about being hit with a pitched ball and charging the mound was very good.

Joaquin threw his first pitch and it did not hit Davis. The pitch was "right down the middle" and Davis belted it so far that it left Wrigley Field. A tremendous home run!

Hendrick was so angry he could not see straight.

He ran toward Joaquin, was quite animated and said, "I thought you were going to drill Jody Davis!"

"I forgot," Joaquin mumbled as he shrugged his shoulders and walked toward the mound.

One tough Dominican.

Lesson 44

There Is Much Help Behind The Scenes

Ron Swoboda and I worked together in 2008, when we broadcast the Triple-A World Series on ESPN2. Swoboda is remembered for making one of the greatest catches in World Series history. When Ron discussed the catch, he was quick to praise Mets coach Eddie Yost.

"Eddie Yost worked with me during the 1968 and '69 seasons. He must have hit eight million balls to me," Ron explained. "I was a terrible outfielder, but thanks to Eddie Yost working with me endlessly, I went from being a complete disaster, to someone who had confidence in himself. We would work on getting my feet right and reading the ball off the bat. The stands at Shea Stadium were very high, so the ball did not come off the bat out in the open sky. Fly balls would get lost in the sea of fans. This was very difficult for a young outfielder. I was really bad. I would call off infielders on fly balls and the balls would drop in for base hits. I also would run into infielders. Fortunately, Bud Harrelson (Mets shortstop) survived."

"During the latter part of the '69 season, I finally convinced our manager, Gil Hodges, not to bring in Rod

Gaspar, as a late inning defensive replacement for me," Ron continued.

Swoboda's hard work and powers of persuasion paid off in Game 4 of the 1969 Fall Classic. The Mets were ahead 1-0 in the ninth inning. Brooks Robinson, of the Baltimore Orioles, was at bat with men at first and third with only one out.

"Robinson lined a ball clearly to my right, and I took the shortest route and most aggressive angle to it," Ron said as he described the play.

Since the potential go ahead run was on first base, many people criticized Ron for diving for the ball. Their feeling was that even though Ron made a great catch, he did not make a smart play.

Swoboda did not see it that way.

"I am not certain there was a safer route to the ball," he said. "The ball was not tailing in my direction."

The runner on third tagged after the catch and scored, while the runner at first was unable to advance. The final out of the inning was recorded with no further scoring and the Mets went on to win the game 2-1.

I have seen the replay of the catch many times. Each time I see it, I cannot believe that Swoboda caught the ball. Ron deserves all the praise he has received for making the catch. Let's tip our cap to Eddie Yost, too.

Lesson 45

Some Home Runs Can Be Bigger Than All Of Us

I haven't seen Pat Darcy since the final day of the 1976 season, although we still to speak to one another by phone a few times each year. Darcy pitched for the Indianapolis Indians for the entire Triple-A season in 1974. Unfortunately, Pat developed shoulder problems and never returned to the Major Leagues, after the Cincinnati Reds optioned him to Indianapolis in June of 1976.

Where was Pat during the 1975 season and the first half of the '76 season?

Ask Carlton Fisk.

Fisk's home run off of Pat in the 12th inning of game six of the 1975 World Series ended one of the greatest games in baseball history. Many people believe <u>that</u> game and <u>that</u> World Series sparked a renaissance in baseball that put "the game" on a path to set attendance records.

I spoke with Pat by telephone in December of '09. We discussed Fisk's home run.

"Pat, do you get asked about the home run often?" I asked.

"Not that much," Pat replied. "I'm always asked about Pete Rose. Pete was very nice to me."

"How did you feel after giving up the home run to Fisk?" I asked Pat.

"I had pitched two scoreless innings prior to giving up the homer," Pat emphatically said. "It was just a loss, one of three losses we had in the Series. If I had given up that home run in game seven, then it would have been a different story."

The Reds overcame a 3-0 deficit in game seven to win their first World Championship in 35 years.

Those of us who witnessed Carlton Fisk's home run at Fenway Park, watched it on television or listened to it on radio, never will forget it.

I will remember Pat Darcy for many reasons besides the Fisk home run. I will remember him because:

- He is a kind, intelligent man with a great sense of humor.
- He is a devoted family man.
- He has been very successful in his post-playing days selling commercial real estate.
- He won 11 games for the Cincinnati Reds during the 1975 season.

I think we all should remember something Carlton Fisk said to Pat Darcy when their paths crossed at a card show more than 25 years later.

"Pat, in the end, that home run was not about you and not about me.

It was bigger than both of us. It was about what it meant to baseball."

Lesson 46

Let Mechanics Work On Cars

Chris Welsh has made a name for himself in the broadcast booth with the Cincinnati Reds. He has been their television analyst for almost two decades. Prior to his broadcast days, Chris pitched professionally for eleven years and spent five seasons in the Major Leagues.

Welsh put up the best numbers of his career with the Indianapolis Indians in 1984. He finished the season 13-4 with a 3.01 ERA. Chris was not pitching poorly in April and May; however, he had too many deep counts and was walking far too many batters. Chris told me that his *mechanics* were not right and they were to blame for those bases on balls.

Buck Rodgers was the Indianapolis Indians manager that year. He became very animated on the subject of Chris Welsh.

"It's not his *mechanics* at all!" Buck said. "He's not pitching aggressively. Chris is walking people because he is nibbling. That will change."

It did. Chris started throwing more first pitch strikes and went on to have a great year.

Pitchers love to talk about their mechanics when

they are not having success. After all, who wants to admit that he is not pitching with confidence. We also should remember that if a man is pitching with hope instead of conviction, his mechanics may suffer.

Lesson 47

The Explanation Is In The Eye Of The Beholder

Jeff Reynolds was the Indianapolis Indians third baseman in 1987. I liked his sense of humor and rarely saw him at a loss for words.

Late in the '87 season, the Indianapolis club was playing in Omaha and battling for first place. Indianapolis was trailing by one run, with two men on and two men out, in the ninth inning. Jeff Reynolds struck out swinging to end the game on a pitch that bounced a great deal in front of home plate. After the game, there was a considerable amount of frustration in the Indians' clubhouse, not only because of the significance of the game, but also because of how it ended. Despite Reynolds' easy-going personality, I am quite certain, he was upset with himself.

The next day, while the players were standing around the batting cage, Omaha Manager Frank Funk was "getting on" Reynolds, whom Funk had managed in winter ball, in Latin America. Frank was relentless in a good-natured way.

"Jeff, how could you swing at a pitch that bounced in the dirt and was so far in front of home plate?" Frank repeatedly asked.

Finally, Reynolds gave his thoughtful and accurate response.

"Everyone on our team is upset because I swung at a pitch that bounced in the dirt," he said. "What these guys should remember, is that the pitch was a foot outside, too."

Lesson 48

Watch Your Words So You Won't Have To Eat Them

Eric Davis came close to becoming the first Major Leaguer to hit 40 home runs and steal 40 bases in the same season. Eric finished the 1987 campaign with 37 homers and 50 stolen bases. He was an excellent player with many accomplishments. Unfortunately, injuries prevented him from reaching his true potential.

When Eric joined the Indianapolis Indians in August of 1983, he received a great deal of fanfare. He was a complete player who was being compared to Willie Mays. Fortunately, Eric had the strength of character not to put undue pressure on himself.

Eric's first game as an Indianapolis Indian was against the Iowa Cubs. He struck out four times and went hitless.

Jim Napier, the Iowa manager, was very pleased with his team's performance that night. His Cubs' had won the game and had shut down Eric Davis. Jim felt good about stopping Davis. *Much too good.*

Jim and I spoke prior to the game the next day. He immediately started talking about Eric.

"They say he can really run. So far we haven't found that out," Napier boasted.

That night Jim Napier found out that Eric Davis could run. Not only that, but Jim also learned that Eric Davis could hit. In fact, everyone in the American Association found those things out, too. In 19 games with the Indianapolis Indians, Eric scored 18 runs and drove in 19 others. He also hit seven homers and stole nine bases.

Great players have a way of humbling the opposition.

Lesson 49

There Are Different Ways Of Saying A Player *Can't Miss*

Harold Baines had an outstanding Major League career. His numbers read as follows: 2,866 hits, 384 home runs and 1,628 runs batted in.

The Chicago White Sox selected Baines with the first overall pick in the 1977 amateur draft. Roland Hemond was the White Sox General Manager at the time and many years later he shared the story of the White Sox decision to draft Baines.

"Our owner, Bill Veeck, told me that he had seen Baines play Little League Baseball on Maryland's eastern shore," Roland said. "Bill said that as a twelve year old Baines had a great swing."

"I am sure that you must have done your homework before drafting him," I said.

"Yes," Roland replied. "Our New England scout Leo Laboisser had seen Baines in a tournament in 1976 and turned in a favorable report. I then sent three other scouts to see Baines play. Benny Huffman, Walter Widmayer and Paul Richards all were assigned to pass judgment."

Scouts have different ways of saying a player will or won't *make it*.

After Paul Richards watched Baines play, Richards spoke with Hemond.

"What do you think of Baines' chances of becoming a solid Major League player?" Roland asked.

"All he has to do is find the ballparks," Paul replied.

I found Richards' words about Baines most insightful and amusing. Harold Baines was THAT talented. And… he "found the ballparks" for more than 20 years.

Lesson 50

Being Critical Of Others Can Create Problems For Yourself

On a rainy May evening during the 1974 season, the Indianapolis Indians and Iowa Oaks were playing at Bush Stadium, in Indianapolis. In the bottom of the sixth inning, in the second game of a doubleheader, Indianapolis had the bases loaded with one out and was trailing by two runs.

The Indians batter, Ken Griffey Sr., grounded a ball to the Iowa first baseman Sam Ewing who fielded it cleanly and took the "sure" out by stepping on first base. Did Ewing have a play at the plate or a play at second base? Yes, on both counts. However, if he had thrown to second base he would have been throwing into the runner. By not throwing to the plate he did not risk a wild throw. Although a run scored on the play, Iowa still had a one run lead, and now there were two men out. You could understand his decision of taking the "sure" out even if you were not completely in agreement with it.

Ewing's teammate, third baseman Lee "Bee Bee" Richard, had a major issue with Sam's decision. Bee Bee repeatedly made his feelings quite clear to Tom Spencer, who had advanced from second to third base on the play.

"That's the dumbest play I've ever seen!" Bee Bee shouted. "What is Sam doing? What is he thinking? Stupidest play I've ever seen!"

Richard continued with his criticism, even when the next batter, Junior Kennedy, came to the plate. Indianapolis now had runners at second and third base with two outs. On the next play, Kennedy grounded a ball right to Richard. Bee Bee fielded the batted ball cleanly and ran to step on third base forgetting that there no longer was a force play.

After Richard realized his mistake, he tried to get the out at first base even though there no longer was a play there. Not only did he make an unnecessary throw, but he threw *wildly*. Both runners scored and Indianapolis won the game!

What's the dumbest play you ever have seen, Bee Bee?

Lesson 51

Business Before Anything Including Patriotism

Mike Jorgensen played both first base and the outfield during his seventeen years in the Major Leagues. In his post-playing days, he has been a Major League Manager, Minor League Manager, Farm Director, Field Coordinator and Scout, all with the St. Louis Cardinals.

Our paths first crossed when Mike managed the Louisville Redbirds, in 1987. Mike told me he loved the challenge of facing great pitchers like Bob Gibson and Tom Seaver. He felt that he had nothing to lose and anything he was able to accomplish was a "big plus."

"Jorgy" was traded five times during his Major League career. Players often are "jolted" the first time they are involved in a trade. They complain that they find out they have been traded by reading the newspaper, listening to the radio, watching television or reading about it on the internet. A player never knows how trade news will be delivered, however, he should find out about it from the teams involved.

On Sunday afternoon, May 22, 1977, Mike would have none of those trade related complaints. The Montreal Expos were at home hosting the San Diego Padres. Mike was quite certain he would play first base since Tony Perez needed a day off. Mike was very surprised to see that Gene Tenace, not he, was to be the Expos first baseman that day.

During the National Anthem, Expos manager Dick Williams called Mike over to the runway leading to the dugout.

"You have been traded to the Oakland A's," Dick said.

During the National Anthem…..During the National Anthem Jorgensen found out he had been traded!

With the game being played in Montreal, both the Canadian and American Anthems were played. This meant that Dick Williams had twice as much time to break the news to Mike.

Mike shared this story with me a few years ago when he was in Indianapolis scouting for the Cardinals. After I shook my head in disbelief, I had a question.

"Which National Anthem, Canadian or American?" I asked.

"I can't remember," he said, with a big smile on his face.

Lesson 52

There Are Different Perspectives On Tardiness

Ron McClain was the Indianapolis Indians trainer from 1973 through 1979. He became the Montreal Expos head trainer in 1980 and served in that capacity for 25 years.

Ron LeFlore originally signed with the Detroit Tigers after serving time in prison for armed robbery. Ron McClain and I first saw LeFlore's tremendous raw speed in 1974, when LeFlore played for Detroit's Triple-A team, the Evansville Triplets. In 1978, with the Tigers, LeFlore led the American League in stolen bases with 68 thefts. Prior to the 1980 season, he was traded to the Montreal Expos and played with them for one year.

Ron McClain shared the following story about Ron LeFlore.

LeFlore was having an excellent season with Montreal (league leading 97 stolen bases) when he ran into a wall, in pursuit of a fly ball, and broke his wrist. He no longer could swing a bat, but he still helped the Expos by pinch running. The Expos and the Philadelphia Phillies were battling for first place in the National League East, so LeFlore's limited participation was very important.

With one week left in the season, the Expos were playing against the Cubs in Chicago. The game started and Ron LeFlore was nowhere to be seen. Ron McClain and the Expos' Brass were extremely concerned about him. *That's putting it mildly.* Finally, in the SECOND INNING, LeFlore arrived at the ballpark. He did not understand why everyone was so worried about his tardiness.

"There's no sense coming early because Dick Williams (Expos Manager) never puts me in the game until the seventh inning, anyway," LeFlore said matter-of-factly.

Lesson 53

You Must Go With Your Strengths

Steve McCatty was named the Washington Nationals pitching coach during the middle of the 2009 season. Prior to getting the Nationals' job, he had been a pitching coach with several teams in the International League.

Steve pitched briefly for the Oakland A's during the 1977 and '78 seasons, and struggled both years. McCatty was a power pitcher. Instead of taking that approach, he was advised to follow scouting reports that suggested he throw a lot of "change-ups" and "breaking balls" to many hitters. It also should be pointed out that in those days, the American League was known as a "breaking ball" League. It's not easy for a young player to openly disagree with his manager or coaches. Steve was following orders and in so doing was not pitching to his strengths.

The turning point in McCatty's career came on May 1, 1979, when the A's were playing the Boston Red Sox in Oakland. Steve was brought in to pitch in the top half of the fifth inning. After getting a ground ball out and issuing an intentional walk, Steve fell behind three balls and no strikes to Red Sox catcher, Bob Montgomery. The bases were loaded and McCatty was a pitch away from walking in a run.

"That's enough of all of these breaking balls and change-ups," Steve mumbled. *"I have to pitch my way."*

McCatty came after Montgomery with three straight fastballs and struck him out swinging. He then got Jerry Remy on a called third strike to end the inning.

Steve became a "Big League" pitcher when he struck out both Montgomery and Remy. He got his first Major League win that day and his confidence was much improved. He won 11 games for Oakland that season and 14 more in each of the next two seasons.

"The change up is a 'feel' pitch," Steve explained. "I can teach it, but I never could throw it."

Lesson 54

Don't Try To Be A Hero

I enjoyed working with Grant Jackson when he was the Indianapolis Indians pitching coach. He had a great feel for pitching. I can understand why he pitched in the Major Leagues for almost twenty years.

Grant was very competitive and when he was young he threw extremely hard. Jackson learned a valuable lesson about pitching during his early days with the Philadelphia Phillies. One day, Grant was facing Willie Mays and threw him a 95 MPH fastball which Willie took for a strike.

"Wow!" Willie exclaimed in his high pitched voice. "You throw hard!"

Willie's words made Grant feel strong and self assured. Grant said to himself that he would throw the next pitch *even harder*. What would Willie say after that one?

Grant reared back and fired. Willie hit the ball well over 400 feet for a home run! Even though Grant was throwing hard, Willie's words of praise were meant to fool Grant, which they did. Willie had *sized up* Grant's fastball.

Grant came to realize that when the pitcher and hitter are both *keyed up,* sometimes the best thing for the pitcher to do is to *take a little something off* his fastball. Grant noted that both the pitcher and hitter want to be heroes in *clutch* situations.

Kansas City Royals Hall of Famer, George Brett said it best,

"Don't try to be a hero. Try to be a winner."

Lesson 55

A Bunt Can Do Wonders

I spent a lot of time with Larry Rothschild when he pitched for the Indianapolis Indians. It became quite apparent to me, that with Larry's baseball knowledge and people skills, he would become a fine pitching coach, someday. Rothschild pitched professionally for eleven seasons and began his coaching career in the Cincinnati Reds' Minor League system in 1986.

Rothschild has been a Major League pitching coach for more than a decade with the Reds, Florida Marlins and Chicago Cubs. In fact, he has been the Cubs' pitching coach under four different managers: Don Baylor, Bruce Kimm, Dusty Baker and Lou Piniella. That should give you an indication of just how knowledgeable and well respected he is among baseball people.

When Rothschild pitched for Indianapolis in the 1970's, I did not have a broadcast partner for road games. There were a lot of doubleheaders in those days. Often, the starting pitcher from the first game would come up to the broadcast booth and join me on the air for the second game. Larry partnered with me on several occasions.

Late in the 1978 season, Larry pitched a shutout against the Evansville Triplets in the first game of a doubleheader. He then made his way to the broadcast booth for the second game.

The second game started in a very positive manner for Indianapolis. Tribe pitcher Dan Dumoulin was mowing the Triplets down, and in the fourth inning the Indians led by two runs. Evansville's Ricky Peters came to bat and Rothschild explained to the listeners that the best thing Peters could do would be to lay down a bunt. Larry pointed out that not only would a bunt hit give the Triplets a much needed base runner, but also it might disrupt Dumoulin's rhythm.

Peters and Rothschild were on the same page. Peters dropped a bunt toward third base and reached base safely. The next three also came through with base hits. Not only was Dumoulin's rhythm gone, but the Triplets came back to win the game.

This was one of many lessons I learned from Larry Rothschild.

Lesson 56

Hitters Bring A Different Perspective

Ted Power has been the Louisville Bats pitching coach for several years. Ted first made it to the Major Leagues, as a player, with the Los Angeles Dodgers, in 1981. Fellow pitchers Jerry Reuss and Terry Forster "showed him the ropes" that season.

"Reuss and Forster taught me how to prepare for a game and how to conduct myself as a Major Leaguer," Ted said. "However, I learned more about pitching from Dusty Baker, than I did from anyone else."

"Dusty Baker, an outfielder?" I asked.

"That's right," Ted responded. "Dusty was with the Dodgers at that time, and he helped me in so many ways. The first thing he taught me was how hitters think. Then he said to always look where hitters have their hands. Study their stances and look at their reactions to pitches. Try to read their bats. See if they make adjustments. Recognize their tendencies."

This is the game within the game.

Ted Power put Dusty Baker's words to good use. Ted pitched in the Major Leagues for almost 13 years. He led the National league in appearances in 1984, with 78, and recorded 27 saves the following season.

Some organizations have made it a point to have pitchers and position players room together in the Minor Leagues. This has enabled pitchers and batters to become more familiar with one another's mindset.

Lesson 57

Savor The Moment

Hank Aguirre was one of the worst hitting pitchers of all time. When Aguirre was a member of the Detroit Tigers, the fans tried to be supportive of him when he batted. Hank would receive applause from the Tiger faithful when he managed to hit a *foul ball*.

I remember watching a game on television, in June of 1967, between the Tigers and the Yankees, at Yankee Stadium. Aguirre came to bat with the bases loaded and Joe Pepitone, the Yankees center fielder, was not exactly *on his toes.*

What do you think happened?

Aguirre hit a ball into the gap in left center field for a triple. I thought something was wrong with my TV. Hank Aguirre had tripled with the bases loaded!

Almost 40 years later, I had the pleasure of meeting former catcher Bill Freehan, a teammate of Aguirre's with the Tigers. Freehan, who was an instructor in the Tigers' Minor League system, was in Toledo working with the Mud Hens catchers.

"Bill," I asked. "Do you remember Hank Aguirre's bases loaded triple at Yankee Stadium?"

Freehan could not contain his laughter.

"Not only do I remember it," Bill said. "Here's the rest of the story. Aguirre got to third base and was greeted by Coach Tony Cuccinello. Cuccinello was just as stunned as everybody else that Aguirre had tripled."

"Tony, what's the steal sign?" Aguirre asked.

"The steal sign!" Tony shouted in disbelief. "Hank, it took you 15 years to get to third base. Why don't you stay here for 15 seconds?"

Lesson 58

Foul Balls Can Put Some People In A Foul Mood

Dave Hollins played in the Major Leagues for more than a decade and now is a scout with the Baltimore Orioles. We spoke at length in Buffalo during the summer of 2009.

"I was with the Phillies in 1993 and we went to Colorado for the first time in late May," Dave said. "The Rockies were an expansion team and we were curious about playing in Denver's high altitude."

Dave Hollins and John (*I'm not an athlete, I'm a baseball player*) Kruk were teammates on the Phillies that season. Hollins was batting behind Kruk on this particular night in late May. Hollins put Kruk in a mighty foul mood during the very first inning. Kruk came to bat with one on and one out and grounded into a force play. *Not a good start* since Kruk, who was not in good shape, had to run in the high altitude.

"The count went to 3-2 on me. Since there were two men out, that meant an automatic start for John at first," Hollins recalled laughing. "I fouled the first pitch back and as Kruk trotted back to first base, he looked at me and muttered something under his breath. Then I fouled off the next pitch, too."

"'You bleeping...' Kruk shouted at me as he again returned to first base," Hollins continued. "Now I have fouled off two 3-2 pitches and I swung at the next pitch and fouled that one, too."

"'You bleeper,'" Kruk screamed at me. "'You bleep.'"

"Everyone was laughing and I did it again. I fouled off another pitch and Kruk went absolutely ballistic," Hollins recalled.

"'If it were me, I would have hit the first pitch fair,'" Kruk screamed at me. "You no good bleeping..."

"By this time Kruk was completely 'out of gas.' There was only one thing I could do to make matters worse for him and I did it!" Hollins said, as he roared with laughter. "I hit a ball into the gap in left center field. John realized he had to score, but he was so exhausted that when he slid it was before he reached home plate. He finally reached out and touched the plate with his left hand. He lay there flat on his back and didn't move for awhile."

Was Kruk able to stay in the game? Not only did he stay in the game, but he rapped out three base hits. *This is precisely how you can be a baseball player without being an athlete.*

Dave Hollins and John Kruk made the All-Star Team that year and the Phillies went on to win the National League Pennant.

Lesson 59

Teamwork Is The Essence Of Life

Throughout baseball history, it has been difficult for Minor League teams to win consecutive championships because of the constant turnover in player personnel. The Indianapolis Indians managed to pull off an incredible feat by winning four straight titles from 1986 – 1989.

Despite all of the roster changes during those years, the Indians were fortunate to have had many *team oriented* players. Baseball, at times, can be a very individualistic sport. However, if you examine championship teams, they possess an element of teamwork that is not found on many losing teams. A player who is focused on winning: hits cut-off-men, runs the bases properly and hits behind runners. There is a big difference between a player who comes to the ballpark with the attitude of, *"What can I do to help my team win today?"* as opposed to one who is only thinking about his own numbers.

Players in the Minor Leagues are not compensated financially for participating in post-season play. There are no Minor League *playoff shares*. In fact, many players in the Minors, who are in their post-season, lose out on some money. They don't get a Major League promotion and subsequent jump in salary until the Minor League playoffs are over.

With that in mind, the Indians' parent team, the Montreal Expos, deserves a great deal of credit. They signed Razor Shines, Alonzo Powell, Casey Candaele, Wally Johnson, Dallas Williams, Billy Moore, Rene Gonzales and others who were very team oriented and offered encouragement to one another.

I asked Razor about those great Indianapolis teams.

"We expected to win," Razor explained. "We constantly talked about winning. All of the young players knew how we felt being *Champions*. Young guys like Randy Johnson and Larry Walker."

Don't misunderstand. Every one of the players wanted to get to the Major Leagues. However, they were determined to play winning baseball while they were in Indianapolis.

The 1986 Indians had a stellar season, while the Montreal Expos did not live up to expectations. During the second half of that season, players jokingly talked about *going UP to Indianapolis and going DOWN to Montreal.*

I interviewed Wally Johnson at Victory Field during the summer of 2009. Wally, who now is a Certified Public Accountant, described his teammates' feelings beautifully.

"We felt that if we did our jobs properly, with the team in mind, getting to the Big Leagues would take care of itself," Wally said.

For the record, Wally Johnson played in the Major Leagues for three full seasons and for parts of six others.

Lesson 60

A Baby's Arrival Can't Be Predicted.

Detroit Tigers Hall of Fame Broadcaster Ernie Harwell and I had a mutual friend named Lloyd Gearhart. Lloyd spent the 1979 season watching games at Bush Stadium, in Indianapolis, while he was scouting for the Yankees.

During the 1946 season, Lloyd and Ernie both were with the Double-A Atlanta Crackers of the Southern Association. Lloyd was an outfielder who later played for the New York Giants and Ernie, a Georgia native, was the Crackers' broadcaster.

At the time, Ernie and Lulu Harwell had a two and a half year old son, named Bill. Lulu was pregnant with the couple's second child.

Ernie and Lulu had a talk with Bill.

"The Lord is going to bring us a baby," they explained to him.

One morning, Lloyd Gearhart decided to visit the Harwell's home. Bill heard a knock and answered the door.

"Is your dad home?" Gearhart asked.

Bill nodded yes.

"Tell your dad, the *Lloyd* is here," Lloyd emphatically said.

Lloyd's words troubled Bill and he frantically rushed to his parents.

"What's the matter, Bill?" Ernie questioned.

"Dad, Dad," Bill replied breathlessly. "The *Lloyd*'s here, but he didn't bring the baby!"

Lesson 61

A "Moose" Can Save The Day

Despite the incredible seasons the New York Yankees were getting from Roger Maris, Mickey Mantle and Whitey Ford in 1961, the Yankees were engaged in quite a pennant race with the Detroit Tigers.

On September 1st, the Tigers came to New York just one and a half games behind the Yankees. I was nine years old and I was pumped up for this three game series!

The series opener was scoreless going into the bottom of the ninth inning. I was watching the game on television with my father.

"After this half inning, you have to go to bed," my father said.

"Dad, the game may go into extra innings," I protested. "There's no score and I really want to see the end of the game."

"Doesn't matter," he emphasized. "Your sister is sleeping and you have to go to bed, too."

He was right. My sister, Elaine, was sleeping. Never mind that she was fourteen months old. I realized that it was pointless to argue with my father. My only hope was that the Yankees would score in the bottom of the ninth.

The inning did not get off to a good start when both Maris and Mantle were retired. There were two outs and nobody on, and I was very upset. However, the inning was not over….Elston Howard and Yogi Berra each singled and up to the plate came Bill "Moose" Skowron. Moose singled to left field scoring Howard and the Yankees won 1-0!

I went to bed *mighty happy* that night. In fact, I went to bed *mighty happy* for the next twelve nights, as the Yankees won thirteen straight to break open the pennant race.

These days, Bill Skowron works in Community Relations for the Chicago White Sox. In 2007, Bob Grim, the White Sox Director of Broadcasting, introduced me to Moose. I shared my story with him and we had a good laugh.

"Do you remember the game and the base hit?" I asked.

"Of course, I do!" Moose replied with emphasis. "When Frank Crosetti (Yankees third base coach) was pretty certain a breaking ball was coming, he would shout, 'Come on Moose!'"

"Before that pitch I heard Crosetti's shout. Don Mossi threw a breaking ball and I 'stayed back' and grounded a single to left field," Moose chuckled.

Moose's base hit put a big smile on my face and I hope the stories in this book put a smile on your face, too.

Acknowledgements

I would like to thank:
Max Schumacher and Cal Burleson for giving me the opportunity to broadcast Indianapolis Indians Baseball.
Every player, coach and manager who has worn an Indianapolis Indians uniform in my years with the team.
Many of the opposing players, coaches and managers. I make it a point to communicate with both the Indians and opposition on a daily basis.
Dennis Kasey for giving me the opportunity to announce baseball on television.
The people who shared their stories for this book.

AuthorHouse Publishers
Brian Bosma, Indianapolis Indians Media Relations Manager
Corbis Corporation
Dan Cooper, Cooper FineArt.com
Indianapolis Public Library
Indianapolis Star
Robin Kellman, back cover photo

My thanks to the following people with whom I have worked in my years in baseball: Tom Akins, Tim Bourff, Brian Dorsett, Carl Erskine, Julie Fischer, Estel Freeman, Brian Giffin, Chris Herndon, Shawn Humphrey,

Indianapolis Indians Front Office, Tommy John, Randy Lewandowski, Scott McCauley, Matt Michael, Dyar Miller, Randy Mobley, Brad Morris, Keith Passon, Robert Portnoy, Branch Rickey III, Karen Robinson, Kim Rogers, Cliff Rubenstein, Scott Rubin, Bruce Schumacher, Mark Schumacher, Matt Segal, Chris Sprague, Dave Streit, Max Stultz, Ron Swoboda, Stuart Tobias, Mark Walpole, Dave West, Mike Wolinsky and Joel Zawacki.

LaVergne, TN USA
11 April 2010
178793LV00001BD/2/P